Earning Admission:

Real Strategies for Getting into Highly Selective Colleges

Greg Kaplan

ISBN-13: 978-1523879168

ISBN-10: 1523879165

To my Mom and Dad, for filling my world with inspiration.

"I never found beauty in longing for the impossible and never found the possible to be beyond my reach." Ayn Rand, *Atlas Shrugged*.

Table of Contents

Introduction

I. I Will Give You the Bad News First: Earning Admission to Highly Selective Colleges Is Hyper Competitive and Biased

Applying to college has become as difficult as winning in Las Vegas. In 2015, high school seniors submitted 244,000 applications to the Ivy League. There were a little more than 14,000 spots for incoming students. That translates to 17.4 applicants for every spot. College deans and admissions officers regularly boast they could fill their entire class with valedictorians and perfect SAT scores. The 244,000 applicants are a tough crowd.

But that is not all...

Applying to highly selective colleges is even worse than the math suggests. Of these 14,000 Ivy League spots, thousands go to recruited athletes, children of generous alumni, and the children of the rich, famous, and powerful. Furthermore, some of the most expensive private high schools in the country have strong ties to selective colleges and regularly send more than half of their senior class to the ivies and other selective colleges. These private schools are not that different from other high-quality high schools across the country. Students attending these schools are buying their way into college by paying $150,000 over four years to attend a high school with an existing relationship with a college or university.

Finally, some of these families hire private college admissions consultants that charge up to $25,000 to help them craft applications that admissions officers want to see. When you add up all of these applicants, there are few spots left for the rest of us.

To make matters even worse (yes, that is possible), many of the most selective colleges in the US have instituted 'no loan' financial aid policies that provide generous grants to attract non-traditional applicants and first-generation college graduates. Many private colleges now are the same price, or even less expensive, than flagship state universities when students factor in the grants they receive. While great for the families of students admitted to these colleges, these policies are making it harder to gain admission. As elite private universities educate the public about their generous financial aid policies, the pool of college applicants continues to grow.

In addition, the number of international applicants for the same precious few spots is also skyrocketing. In 2013, 886,052 foreign students enrolled in US undergraduate and graduate programs, representing a 72% increase from 2000. 31% of these students hail from China, where competition for spots at Chinese universities is even fiercer than in the United States. Now your child is competing against an ever-increasing pool of talented students from all over the world.

The competition extends far beyond the Ivy League. Nationwide, the number of applicants to the top public and private universities continues to skyrocket. In 2014, there were 86,554 applicants for the 5,800 spots in the freshman class at UCLA. Crosstown rival USC received 51,800 applicants for 2,750 spots.

The college admissions process is even more competitive than you thought.

II. Now the Good News: Your Child Can Compete and Earn Admission with Strategy and Marketing

Unlike Las Vegas, this is not a gamble—this is your child's future. While there are no guarantees in this process, you can maximize your child's odds of gaining admission in this competitive process through strategic planning and marketing.

Planning sets your child up for success...

When your child applies to college, she will have three years of grades behind her and either a SAT or ACT score. You must ensure that your child's high school transcript and entrance exam scores are competitive for the admissions process. Through planning and strategy, you can ensure that your child has the necessary grades and SAT/ACT scores to be a competitive applicant. Your child will need to take classes he will earn A's in. If your child will earn an 'A' in Spanish IV, or a 'B' in AP Spanish if she skips Spanish IV, Don Quixote can wait one more year, and your child can maintain the grades she needs for Cornell. Planning that starts before your child's freshman year can help create the perfect transcript needed for admission.

Finding the right SAT or ACT tutor or prep program can help your child understand how these tests work and how to achieve a competitive score. The SAT and ACT favor the prepared. There are a few natural test takers out there who score incredibly well right off the bat. I was not one of them. Odds are your child, as smart as she is, is not one of them either. With hundreds of thousands of applicants, the right test prep program can make the difference between admission and rejection.

Planning alone is not enough; demonstrating and marketing your child's value to a college admissions officer will separate her from the other 200,000+ applicants.

Given the competition and preferences for recruited athletes and children of alumni and future donors, it should come as little surprise that perfect grades and SAT scores are not enough to gain admission to a selective college. At my welcome speech at Penn, the Dean boasted that Penn received enough candidates with perfect SAT scores to fill the entire freshman class.

To gain admission, your child will need to stand out from the rest of the applicants. Every essay she writes, major she selects, and activities she lists on her application are an opportunity to convince an admissions officer to admit her. Your child must use every component of the college application process to demonstrate that she will bring value to the college she wants to attend—value that sets her apart from the other applicants. College is a time for students to discover their passions and add to the learning of other students. A demonstrated leader with a passion in a particular field may have an easier time gaining acceptance than a student that joined countless activities in high school but was unfocused. Students who can demonstrate maturity and perspective will fare better than those who come off as self-important. Said differently, every essay your child writes needs to demonstrate her ability to contribute to her 'dream' college.

III. Demonstrate Your Child's Value to a College Admissions Officer to Earn Admission

Earning Admission is designed to teach you and your child the mindset for creating an application that stands out by anticipating what college admissions officers are looking for:

- Strong academic performance and entrance exam scores.
- A cohesive theme that ties the entire application together.
- Personal statements highlighting experiences or perspectives that show your child's ability to contribute value to her 'dream' college.
- Achievements in extracurricular activities that your child will continue in college.

The college admissions process is a stacked game. In Las Vegas, the house wins. Here, the favored applicants will continue to gain admission. By using strategy and marketing in your child's applications you can maximize your child's odds of earning admission. Give the admissions officer what they want to see, and your child will stand out.

IV. *Earning Admission's* Approach to Gaining Admission

There are several components of the college application that your child will use to earn admission including:

(1) High school transcript;

(2) SAT/ACT scores;

(3) Personal statement;

(4) Responses to application form questions;

(5) Extracurricular activities including sports, art, and internships;

(6) Letters of recommendation; and

(7) Depending on the college, admissions interviews.

Each component must work together with the other components and should be viewed as opportunity to persuade an admissions officer to offer admission to your child. Your child must assemble an application that ties together all of your child's strengths and create a convincing case for an admissions officer to admit your child.

The college admissions process has dramatically changed from when you applied to college. It may help to compare the college application to a job application. Why does an employer hire one job applicant over any other?

To earn admission, your child must convince an admissions officer that she will contribute value to that college. For some applicants that is easier than others. A world-class athlete will have little trouble convincing a college to admit her. The prospect of a national championship or league title is all it takes. Admissions officers see dollar signs with the child of a hedge fund manager or third generation alumni.

For the rest of us, persuading an admissions officer and committee to accept a student is more nuanced. *Earning Admission* explores each component in detail and what an applicant can do to create a compelling application that convinces an admissions officer to admit an applicant. *Earning Admission* is written to get you and your child to approach the college application process from the perspective of the college admissions officer.

IV. How *Earning Admission* Is Structured

Earning Admission discusses each component of the college application:

Part I explores the objective components, which are assessed with fixed criteria like grades and scores. These components include the high school transcript and entrance exams.

Part II explores the subjective components, which are open to interpretation by admissions officers. These components include personal statements, extracurricular activities, letters of recommendations, responses to application form questions, and interviews.

Each of the components below is presented from the perspective of the college admissions officer:

1. **High school transcript**:
   Can your child handle the coursework at my college or university? Will she be able to succeed and contribute to the academic environment? Has she taken challenging courses that have prepared her for Harvard, Stanford, Duke, etc.? If the answer is no, I am going to put the application down.

2. **SAT/ACT scores**:
   How can I tell if Any Town USA High School prepared applicants for my college in the same way as my favorite, Fancy Boarding School, from which we accepted 25 students last year? I need some

objective criteria to evaluate the academic potential of Suburban Public High School vs. Expensive Urban Elite Prep School. I am going to pretend all SAT takers are created equal and not believe some parents pay $350 per hour for their children to learn to master the test.

3. **Personal Statement**:
   I am looking for interesting students with perspective that will add to my college's culture and enrich the learning experience for all. I love to see an applicant that has perspective and an understanding of why she wants to go to Tufts. The next student who tries to portray herself as Mother Theresa because she did Habitat for Humanity and fifteen other community service clubs will make me scream.

4. **Responses to application form questions (i.e. major choice):**
   It is refreshing to see a female applicant applying as a Biochemistry major; we receive far more male applicants in that field. The School of Nursing at Penn receives less male applicants than female applicants. Odd, the School of Human Ecology at Cornell gets fewer applicants than our other schools. Why did half the class apply as Psychology or Economics majors? We need a well-rounded student body!

5. **Extracurricular Activities:**
   Junior is a great lacrosse player. That is okay, but our lacrosse team has too many lacrosse players to choose from. What we really need is help filling the squash team and women's crew team. Wow, Susie started a 501(c)(3) nonprofit that is consistent with her goal to do cancer research when she graduates. She is going to be successful here at Pomona.

6. **Letters of Recommendation:**
   Billy's teacher was able to provide great insight into his ability to help his classmates and that he wants to study computer science.

It is great when the recommenders know enough about the student to write an insightful recommendation.

7. **Interview:**
Our alum wrote a nice letter about Maria and why she wants to attend Washington University in St. Louis. I'll consider this letter if Maria's application comes down to wire.

Finally, the part that ties the entire application together and which must be considered for every component:

Theme:
There isn't a catch-line for the applicant to write it down anywhere, but I get it: Tommy is an aspiring engineer who will become fluent in Spanish at Johns Hopkins and is committed to improving Latin America. He is going to really add to our college and everything he has done has prepared him for joining us at Johns Hopkins.

Part III of *Earning Admission* focuses on how your child can improve her odds of admission and reduce the cost of her college education. Each Chapter in Part III discusses application strategy for selecting the colleges your child will apply to, the timing of your child's applications to increase her odds of admission, maximizing merit scholarships and need-based grants, and earning admission from the waitlist.

VI. Who *Earning Admission* Is Addressed to

Earning Admission is addressed to an applicant's parents. That is not to say a high school student should not read this book and implement its advice on her own. I encourage high school students to read this guide and adopt its framework for succeeding in the fiercely competitive college application process. But parent and child alike may ask: well, why is this addressed to mom or dad extraordinaire and not the standout student?

First, addressing this book to the parents of talented and driven college applicants is recognition, that you, the parent, are the most instrumental force in your child's life in preparing her for college. Earning admission to Northwestern does not begin with a high school senior's straight 'A' transcript, perfect SAT score and compelling essay. To the student reader: you should celebrate your achievements, but recognize that your success began much earlier than you may think.

Parents—your child may be the greatest reflection of your own self. Your child's success began with the passion for life and learning you instilled from the very beginning. Your child's success comes from the guidance and direction you provided, the countless edits on book reports, questions on geometry problems and, most importantly, the confidence you inspired in your child. Take a deep breath—your child will succeed. If your biggest concern as a parent at the moment is whether your child will be admitted to Stanford or Cornell, your child is already successful.

Second, the college application process is a family affair that you will likely need to spearhead. Regardless of whether your child is enrolled in public or private high school, do not trust guidance counselors to help your child earn acceptance into college. An example from my own life: I attended one of the top public high schools in California that regularly sends over twenty students to the Ivy League plus dozens more to the most selective colleges, including Stanford and Northwestern, each year. My assigned guidance counselor was responsible for assisting me to navigate the college application process.

In September of my senior year, I met with her to discuss my college plans. Before I could even tell her where I wanted to apply, she told me that I should save my parents a lot of money and just go to the local community college and then transfer to a University of California ("UC") campus. Odd, she seemed put off when I handed her a stack of guidance counselor recommendation forms and an early decision application to Princeton.

This is not just a public school problem—I have heard similar stories from parents whose kids attend "prestigious" private school as well. The most important takeaway from this guide is that you must make sure your child is on the path to acceptance because it is likely no one else going to do that for your child.

My experience applying to college—completely alone and with no guidance—is the genesis of my desire to help you and your child navigate a biased admission process, earn admission, and beat the odds. Your child can do it; a little help from you can go a long way.

Third, the application process begins in earnest in ninth grade. Your child will be thirteen or fourteen years old and most likely too young to appreciate the path that she is on. You will need to make sure your child is earning the best grades she can. You will need to make sure she is enrolled in honors, accelerated and advanced placement courses when appropriate. You will be the one interviewing SAT tutors and driving your child to games and events where she will develop her value in the eyes of a college admissions officer. The task of ensuring your child succeeds is in your court.

Fourth, parents may need to provide guidance in the application process. You know your child better than anyone. Would she be happy in a city or 3,000 miles from home? You will also have to evaluate your child's application materials. Does her essay on finding her passion for building things and a desire to become an engineer that stems from a habitat for humanity outing in eleventh grade, resonate with you? Is your daughter, who aspires to study biochemistry in college, participating in the right internship at the local university during the summer? You may be the only sounding board in the application process, and the only set of eyes reviewing her application for typos, that truly cares about the quality of her personal statement.

Finally, you may assist your child in whole or part with financing the cost of her education. Some may disagree on this, especially a headstrong seventeen year old, but footing all or part of the bill gives you a seat at the table. If you will be paying for college, you have a vested interest in making sure your child creates compelling college applications that translate into acceptances and, potentially, merit scholarships.

VII. One Final Thought Before You Begin

The college application process can be stressful, but take a deep breath knowing that you are doing everything you can and should to maximize your child's odds of acceptance. Look forward to spending time with your child before she moves 3,000 miles away from home and breaks the promise to call home every night.

Looking back to the college application process, I would be lying if I told you that I did not remember the panic attack associated with finding out one of my recommenders did not submit her letters by the deadline, or the hours (I mean *hours*) I spent studying for the SAT. Those moments were not so great. But, I also remember the good times in the process like getting lost with my mom in Philadelphia, trying to find Penn's campus— with no one willing to help—until we decided we didn't feel safe and blew off my eventual alma mater for a trip to the mall. We still laugh about getting into a college that we couldn't find on a map. There is hope for everyone.

When I reflect about applying to college, I do not think about the SAT, the applications, the acceptances and rejection letters, or anything about applying to college for that matter. I think back to the kitchen table talks with my family, where I felt anything was possible and everything was unknown. Parents, cherish the growing experience that your child is going through as she learns how to reflect upon herself, distill her accomplishments and market her value to a targeted audience. Your child is learning how to succeed in the world. There is a reason why the college application process coincides with your child becoming a young adult.

I wish you and your child the best of luck.

PART I:

Maximizing The Objective Components Of The College Application

Part I of *Earning Admission* discusses the objective parts of your child's college application: the high school transcript and college entrance examination (SAT or ACT) scores. It provides you with the mindset you need to maximize your child's high school grades with the goal of gaining admission to highly selective colleges. Part I also provides you with guidance on approaching the college entrance examinations and ensuring your child is prepared to score as high as possible on them and ensure that she is a competitive applicant for the colleges she would like to attend.

Your child should aim for the best possible GPA and entrance exam scores. You and your child can use smart planning, resources available through her high school, and private tutoring to maximize her GPA and SAT/ACT scores. Your job as parent is to ensure that your child is positioned to succeed in high school and when she takes the SAT/ACT. The high school transcript and SAT/ACT scores your child uses in her college application take years to earn. The earlier you focus on these application components and plan for your child's success, the better your child will do. When it comes to college applications, fortune favors the prepared.

Chapter 1:

The High School Transcript

I. The High School Transcript: the Most Important Part of the College Application

Your child's high school transcript is the most important part of her college application. It shows the classes your child has taken in high school, her performance in them, whether she challenged herself with advanced or honors classes, and is the best indicator of your child's ability to succeed in college. It reflects your child's work ethic and preparation for more difficult, college-level courses.

As I mentioned in the introduction, the most selective colleges in the country could fill their entering freshman class with valedictorians. Even though the high school transcript is very important, a straight 'A' transcript is not enough to persuade an admissions officer to admit your child. Think of the high school transcript as the first step for your child to be seriously considered for admission. With so many applicants, it's not possible to get past the first hurdle with lackluster grades. A strong high school transcript will make your child competitive and lead admissions officers to spend more time evaluating other components of her application.

Your child's high school transcript is an opportunity to prove that she will be able to handle a more rigorous college curriculum and contribute to the learning of the entire college. To do this, your child will need to secure straight 'A's' or as close to straight 'A's' as possible. From making sure your child takes classes that provide her with the strongest chance of earning an 'A', to finding tutors or afterschool homework help, you can support your child in crafting a compelling high school transcript.

II. What Admissions Officers Look for in the High School Transcript.

When a college admissions office receives more than 50,000 applicants, it automatically rejects many of the applicants whose grades are not competitive. They look to the applicants' high school performance to cull the herd in a relatively easy way. When evaluating an application, admissions officers ask:

1. Did an applicant excel in her classes?

In a hyper competitive environment, colleges have the luxury of admitting applicants who have excelled in their high school courses. Perfect grades are the norm at colleges like Williams or UCLA. With so many applicants, college admissions officers look to the cream of the crop for their incoming classes.

2. Is the applicant prepared for university coursework?

College courses are typically much more challenging and faster paced than high school classes. Admissions officers seek students who can handle the courses at their college and contribute to their classmates' learning. Admissions officers will assess whether an applicant has taken the necessary courses (i.e. four years of English, Calculus, a foreign language, three years of physical science, etc....) that ensure she is prepared for their college.

3. Did the applicant challenge herself?

Obtaining a college degree will require your child to challenge herself and work hard. While it is true that 'C's' earn degrees in college, admissions officers do not want to admit students who will coast through college. Admissions officers want to admit students who will contribute to the college during their studies and take advantage of the opportunities for higher learning. Therefore, admissions officers will assess whether your child took advantage of opportunities to challenge herself at her high school. As part of the application process, admissions officers receive reports listing the honors and advanced placement courses that were offered at your child's high school. They will know whether your child pushed herself or coasted. To be competitive, your child must push herself with the classes she takes in high school AND do very well in them.

4. Is the student well rounded?

Even if your child intends to apply to specific college program like engineering, admissions officers recognize that well-rounded college students are more successful in their chosen field because they draw on a wide variety of interests and experiences. Admissions officers want to see that your child is challenging herself in different subject areas that will make her a well-rounded college student. Moreover, as people study and work in an increasingly international environment, admissions officers will assess whether your child is developing proficiency in a foreign language. Admissions officers will also assess if your child has developed the ability to problem solve and communicate effectively.

III. Creating a Compelling High School Transcript

Your child needs to do two things to make her transcript competitive for the college application process at highly selective colleges:

(1) Take advanced courses; and

(2) Do well in them.

Your child needs to earn as many 'A's' as possible to be competitive for highly selective colleges. When your child applies for college, her transcript will be already set and cannot be changed. Planning, beginning in ninth grade, is crucial to maximize the value of your child's transcript. To set your child up for success, consider the following:

1. *Find out your child's high school grading policy.*

Different high schools and school districts have different rules about what grade actually appears on the high school transcript. Some schools round off any pluses or minuses so only an 'A' or 'B' appears on a transcript. With these schools, straight 'A-'s' would be fine for your child, as a college admissions officer would only see the 'A's'. Other schools show the pluses and minuses and your child will need to make sure she earns 'A's', not just 'A-'s'.

2. *Your child must take honors and advanced classes.*

Highly selective colleges look for the best and brightest from hundreds of thousands of applicants. Make sure your child is among the best and brightest by enrolling your child in her high school's honors and advanced placement/international baccalaureate programs. Honors programs can start as early as seventh or ninth grade.

3. *Adopt a defensive mindset: 'A's' are your child's to lose.*

There is no grading curve in high school. Your child can earn an 'A' in every one of her classes if she does well. You must be an engaged parent and make sure your child is on track to earn an 'A' throughout the entire semester. Does your child need to meet with her teacher after school? Make sure she does. Some fourteen and fifteen-year-olds need positive reinforcement from home to make sure they are on track for success. Your child is still a child, and you are responsible for her academic performance. Does your child need private tutoring in Physics or Calculus? It is okay if she does—these are difficult subjects. Help your child find the resources she needs that fit within your budget.

4. *Your child should not be in a rush to take the most advanced classes offered at her high school.*

Your child may have the option to take either Pre Calculus (Honors) in her junior year of high school or Advanced Placement Calculus. If math is not your child's strongest subject and she will struggle to earn an

'A', it makes more sense for your child to take her time with Pre Calculus (Honors), earn an 'A' and then take AP Calculus in her senior year and earn an 'A' in that class instead of settling for a 'B' in AP Calculus in her junior year. Part of your defensive strategy is to make sure your child takes courses she can excel in. Consider the following two examples:

Math: your child has the option to take Pre Calculus Honors or Advanced Placement Calculus AB after completing Algebra II Honors.

Option 1:

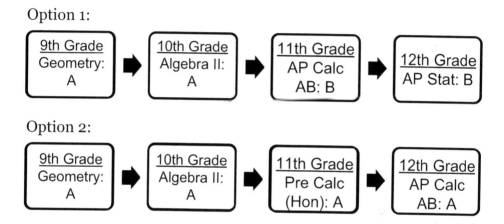

Option 2:

Here, Option 2 is better because it provides your child the opportunity to build her skill set in math at a pace where she will earn straight 'A's'. Play to your child's strength with the subjects that she is the strongest in. If your child is stronger in English than Math, have her push with advanced History and English classes that boost her GPA, and maintain a defensive position in subjects that are more of a challenge for her, like math and science.

Spanish: consider an additional example for Spanish where a student can either take Spanish IV or Advanced Placement Spanish Language after completing Spanish III.

Option 1:

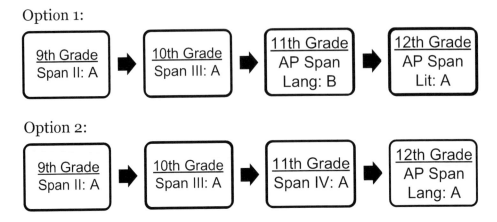

Option 2:

Here, like the first example with math, Option 2 is better because your child can earn 'A's' throughout her entire high school Spanish career by setting a pace that she can excel in. Remember that your child will likely be enrolled in multiple advanced placement and/or honors courses at the same time. Your child should take as many advanced or accelerated courses as possible in which she is able to earn 'A's'. However, if your child has too many honors or advanced courses on her plate, her performance could suffer. Pick and choose classes wisely based on your child's strengths. Stack the playing field to give your child the advantage to earn 'A's.'

5. *Do your homework: find the easy 'A' advanced courses that play to your child's strength.*

We all know some classes are just easier than others. At my high school, AP European History was a much easier 'A' to earn than AP Physics—especially for someone like me who hated Physics. I took AP European History, earned an 'A', and avoided a likely 'B' in AP Physics. If your child's school won't tell you what courses are relatively easier for earning an 'A', either ask parents of older students, or have your child find out from older students. Remember, your child must take as many advanced courses as possible and earn as many 'A's' in them to be competitive in the college application process. Avoid unnecessarily tough teachers that are terrible graders, if possible. Find the classes in your child's high school in which she can earn 'A's', boost her GPA, and position herself as a competitive applicant.

IV. How to Set Your Child Apart from the Other Applicants

1. *Demonstrate success in your child's chosen area of study.*

In addition to your child earning as many 'A's' as she can with an advanced course load, your child can also differentiate herself based on her own interests. If your child plans to apply as an engineering major, make sure she has demonstrated an ability to excel in engineering-related subjects by enrolling in advanced chemistry, physics, and math classes that are offered at her high school.

2. *Take advantage of opportunities to take college courses during high school.*

If your high school allows your child to take courses at a college either during the semester or during the summer for class credit, consider it as an additional opportunity for your child to shine and stand out from applicants that only take high school courses. Colleges ask applicants to list any college courses they have completed in the application process. Your child will have to do well in these courses, but completing college-level courses in high school will set her apart from the other applicants by demonstrating her ability to already excel at this more advanced level.

3. *Give colleges what they are looking for: foreign language proficiency.*

Many highly selective universities have a foreign language requirement as part of the application process and as a graduation requirement. This is the higher education world's recognition that we live in an increasingly interconnected world where graduates will work abroad with people from different backgrounds and need to understand different cultures. Since colleges want their graduates to develop proficiency in a foreign language by the time they graduate from college, your child can demonstrate she will meet a college's goal by developing this proficiency in high school. Consider widely spoken languages used in business like Spanish or Mandarin. Proficiency in these languages will not only benefit your child's college application, but also dramatically improve her future job or graduate school prospects.

V. Conclusion

With hundreds of thousands of applicants vying for relatively few spots at highly selective colleges, your child must apply to college from a position of strength with stellar high school grades. Be prepared to help your child earn 'A's' in every single class and to take as many advanced courses as she can handle. A strong high school transcript will make your child competitive in the college application process and give admissions officers a reason to read the other components of her college application.

Chapter 2:

Entrance Exam Scores

I. Entrance Exams: the Higher the Score, the Higher Likelihood Your Child Will Be Admitted.

College admissions offices claim to take a 'holistic' approach to evaluating applicants. The numbers suggest otherwise: students with higher SAT and ACT scores are admitted at a higher rate than students with lower scores. After your child's high school transcript, your child's SAT or ACT scores are the second most important part of her college application.

You may ask how an admissions officer compares the rigors of your child's high school to another high school. While admissions officers receive reports listing a high school's advanced placement course offerings and college matriculation rate, there is no way to assess how prepared your child will be compared to a child from any other high school. College admissions officers use entrance exams as an objective way to measure an applicant's preparation for college. With so many applicants, college admissions officers have the luxury of accepting candidates with the best scores.

1. What is the SAT and ACT?

The SAT I and the ACT are aptitude tests. The organizations that administer these tests claim that they assess how well the test takers analyze and solve problems. These organizations claim that these tests measure literacy and writing skills that are needed for academic success in college. The tests are administered under a tight time limit to help produce a range of scores.

Whether these tests are fair and accurate, or merely create unnecessary anxiety for both test takers and their parents, is open for debate. What is certain is that college admissions officers give great weight to these scores as part of the college application process. For your child to be competitive in the application process, she must receive a score that places her at the top of the applicant pool.

What is the difference between the SAT and ACT? SAT stands for the Scholastic Aptitude Test and tests a student's ability to reason in writing, critical reading and math. ACT stands for American College Testing and tests a student's ability to reason in English, Math, Reading, Science, and Writing (optional, but most likely required by colleges your child plans to apply to). The decision to take the SAT I or the ACT comes down to your child's personal preference and whether the colleges your child wishes to attend accept them. The SAT II's are subject tests that assess what your child has learned in that subject area. They will be discussed shortly.

SAT I and ACT		
Entrance Exam:	SAT I	ACT
Time:	3 hr + 50 min optional essay	4 hr
Subjects Tested:	1. Math; 2. Evidence Based Reading and Writing; 3. Essay (optional)	1. Math; 2. Reading; 3. English; 4. Science; 5. Writing (optional)
Component Score Range:	200 - 800	1 - 36
Total Score Range:	400 - 1600	1 - 36

II. What Admissions Officers Look for with the SAT/ACT

The SAT (I and II) or ACT scores your child receives are presented as a number. There is nothing personal about them. Admissions officers will compare your child's scores to those of tens of thousands of other applicants. The higher your child's scores, the more competitive your child will be as an applicant.

As previously discussed, many of the most selective colleges in the country could fill their entire freshman class with applicants who have perfect SAT or ACT scores. Strong SAT or ACT scores do not make your child a great college student but strong SAT or ACT scores will lead admissions officers to spend more time looking at the rest of your child's application.

III. What You Must Do With the SAT/ACT

1. Understand the SAT/ACT: the higher the score, the higher the rate of admission

When it comes to the SAT or ACT, your child needs to be competitive with the other applicants. Colleges publish data on their previous year's applicants' SAT and ACT scores. For example, Brown University published the following information about the SAT I Math scores from the 2014 applicant pool on its admissions webpage:

Brown University SAT I Math Scores Distribution					
Score %	**Applied**	**Accepted**	**Accepted%**	**Enrolled**	**% of Class**
800	3,284	535	16%	233	20%
750-790	4,643	617	13%	337	29%
700-740	4,108	479	12%	265	23%

Brown University SAT I Math Scores Distribution					
Score %	Applied	Accepted	Accepted%	Enrolled	% of Class
650-690	3,946	308	8%	198	17%
600-640	2,459	142	6%	100	9%
550-590	1272	25	2%	18	2%
<550	1,106	11	1%		

As you can see, the admissions rate at Brown was significantly higher (although still low) for perfect SAT scores when compared to scores below 700.

Other colleges publish a 25% and 75% range for the SAT and ACT scores they receive. For example, the 2014 Claremont McKenna applicant pool SAT Critical Reading component 25th percentile was 660 and the 75th percentile was 750. This means that of all the applicants, 75% scored a 660 or higher, and the top 25% of the applicant pool scored 750 or higher. Keep in mind that Claremont McKenna had an 11% acceptance rate in 2014. Many students who scored in the top 25% for this SAT component were not accepted.

Do not interpret this data to mean that a higher SAT score automatically translates to earning admission. An applicant who scores an 800 on the SAT I Math component may also be performing very well in her high school classes as well. This data suggests that students with higher SAT scores are admitted at significantly higher rates than students with lower SAT scores. Part II of *Earning Admission* will give your child the tools to persuade an admissions officer to admit her once she has the grades and entrance exam scores that make her a competitive applicant.

A word of caution: you may look at the range of scores and see that applicants are admitted with lower entrance exam scores. Yes, some lower

32

scoring applicants are accepted to highly selective universities. Of the relatively few students at the low end of the spectrum who are accepted, many are recruited athletes and other favored applicants (children of alumni, donors, or very well-connected applicants). Your child will have a much harder time gaining admission to her dream college with SAT or ACT scores which are not at the top of the range.

Your job as a parent is to set your child up for success with the SAT or ACT, thereby ensuring that admissions officers seriously consider the rest of her application.

2. *Figure out where your child stands early on by taking the PSAT and PLAN exams*

Your child should take the PSAT in October of her sophomore year of high school and again in her junior year of high school. Every October, the College Board (the organization that administers the SAT) offers the PSAT (pre-SAT). The PSAT is offered to high school juniors in October as part of the National Merit Scholarship Program (top performers are eligible for large scholarships) and to introduce the SAT to future college applicants. The PSAT is structured like the SAT, with similar time constraints, and consists of a math, verbal, and an English grammar section like the SAT.

PSAT test takers receive a score that is not reported to colleges for admissions purposes. By taking the PSAT sophomore year, your child will gain familiarity with the SAT early in high school with no risks. Through your child's PSAT score report, you can identify your child's strengths and weaknesses with the exam, and adopt the appropriate test prep program that works for your family and child.

Your child may also have the option to take the PLAN test during sophomore year of high school as well. Like the PSAT, the PLAN is the non-reported diagnostic exam for the ACT. Your child should take this exam. Some students prefer either the SAT or the ACT. The PSAT and PLAN will help your child identify if she prefers one test instead of the other and will be used as a starting point in the test preparation process.

Save the score reports from the PSAT and PLAN. Your child will use them to prepare for the SAT or ACT to identify areas needing improvement. If your child scores in the same range on both the PSAT and the PLAN, the decision to take either the SAT or the ACT will be influenced by the availability of test prep programs in your area, which colleges your child is interested in applying to and their preferences as to the entrance exam.

3. *Implement a test prep program*

To be a competitive applicant, your child must be at the top of the applicant pool with respect to entrance exam scores. If your child is not initially scoring in the top 25% of the applicant pool for the colleges she is interested in, you *must* implement a test prep program to improve her scores.

There are a variety of test prep programs that can help your child improve her entrance exam scores. Your child can use an independent study program, a group class, or a private tutor. Private tutors will be the most expensive. The more hands-on and individual attention your child receives, the more expensive the prep program will be.

You may ask, what is the right test prep program for my child? The answer is whatever program helps her score in the top 25% of the applicant pool for the college your child wants to attend. Only you and your child, together, can answer what prep program that is. The SAT and ACT can be mastered. Your student can learn techniques for specific types of questions that previously seemed impossible to answer. By the end of my SAT prep program, I knew the answer for some math questions without even needing to read them. I scored a perfect 800 on the Sat I Math component. Find a program that gives your child that outcome within your budget and make sure she sticks with it.

Both college and the college application process are shockingly expensive. Personally, I found it a bitter pill to swallow paying for a private SAT tutor, knowing that I would pay a fortune to attend college the following year. However, I knew that I did not have the SAT scores needed to get into the colleges I wanted to attend. SAT tutoring was one of the best investments my family made in me to this day. I went from a 660 on the SAT I Math component to an 800 and raised my other SAT I component and SAT II scores as well. Private tutoring paid off immensely in the form of acceptances I probably would not have otherwise received. Prioritize SAT prep above anything else.

When evaluating tutors or other test prep programs, ask to discuss their track records. Ask about their prior students' starting scores—especially in the range your child is starting at—and how they scored after the prep program. My SAT tutor gladly shared her outcomes, good and bad, and warned me that she would fire me as a client if I did not keep up with the assignments. I needed the discipline only a private tutor could provide.

Begin your search for a SAT prep program early. It may take longer than it should. It is sad, but from my own experience, do not expect friends to share with you their child's coveted SAT tutor. After all, your child is competing with their child. Several of my classmates (including friends I grew up with and played on a travelling basketball team with) had used a particular SAT tutor. I heard second-hand how they had scored remarkably well on the SAT and asked them if they used a SAT tutor, but both they, and several other classmates who I had known for years, remained tight-lipped. Eventually, a friend of mine who had aced the SAT, and felt more confident in her own admissions prospects, divulged the name of the tutor!

4. *Begin a test prep program either the second half of sophomore year or the summer prior to junior year to be ready for the PSAT and SAT junior year.*

Preparing for the SAT or ACT can be a long and time-consuming process. Both tests measure aptitude, or the ability to think and solve problems. These skills are not class concepts your child can memorize. Your child will have to learn the mindset of the SAT and ACT tests to score very well. Your child will need an ample amount of time to prepare.

Summer is a great time to begin preparing for college entrance exams because a prep program will not interfere with you child's schoolwork.

By starting test prep early, your child will have more time to master the skills of understanding the test questions and developing the thought process to easily find the correct answer. You will also have ample time to evaluate your child's progress and determine if your child needs to change her test prep strategy. Your child should be prepared to take the SAT or ACT by the end of her junior year of high school.

If your child needs to take the test a second or third time, she will have additional opportunities to do so in the fall of her senior year. College admissions officers consider your child's best score. Most colleges use the best scores for each individual component across all the tests your child has taken, while others consider the best combined score from one test date. Regardless of the college's policy on using the best individual components or combined test scores, your child can take the test again, and use a higher score for her college application.

Your child's academic performance cannot suffer at the expense of SAT prep. Your child must excel with both her high school grades and college entrance exams to be a competitive applicant. Starting early and using the summer(s) for test prep can alleviate the pressure of studying for classes and the SAT at the same time.

An additional benefit of starting SAT prep either during sophomore year or the summer after will include preparing for the PSAT in October of your child's junior year. The PSAT is the test that high school juniors take for the National Merit Scholarship Program. Juniors who score at the top of the PSAT pool will be eligible for significant scholarships at prestigious and selective universities (not Ivy/Ivy equivalents, but some very selective colleges nonetheless). Each year, 3,900 students receive scholarships through the National Merit Scholarship program directly from colleges. Many other scholarships are awarded from corporate sponsors as well.

5. *SAT II Subject Tests*

Many selective colleges require applicants using the SAT I as part of their college application to also take at least two additional SAT II subject tests. Yes, I know what you are thinking—*there is a SAT I and a SAT II?* Yes, it is true. However, unlike the SAT I, the SAT II is an hour-long content-based test designed to assess a student's achievement in specific subject areas. For me, the SAT II's were a much more pleasant experience.

SAT II Subject Tests		
Humanities	**Math and Science**	**Foreign Language**
Literature	Math Level 1	Spanish
U.S. History	Math Level 2	Spanish with Listening
World History	Biology/EM	French
	Chemistry	French with Listening
	Physics	German
		German with Listening
		Modern Hebrew
		Italian
		Latin
		Chinese with Listening
		Japanese with Listening
		Korean with Listening

Preparing for the SAT II subject tests is different than preparing for the SAT I because the SAT II tests content, not reasoning skills. Guidebooks can reinforce concepts your child will have already learned by studying a particular subject area in school. Your child prepares during the entire school year for the SAT II. Your child simply needs to make sure she is familiar with all of the material that could be tested and knows how to apply any of the concepts that will be tested.

Your child should take the SAT II subject tests at the end of the academic year in which she is enrolled in the subject. Your child should take the SAT II in every subject she studies in high school that she is confident she will do well in. A general rule of thumb is that if your child is enrolled in an advanced placement, international baccalaureate, or honors class, she will be sufficiently prepared to take the SAT II test in that subject area if she supplements her classes with guide books to fill in any gaps/bolster any weak areas. Colleges use the best scores on the SAT II's for the college application, so your child should take SAT II's in subjects she feels confident with. This means avoiding tests in your child's weaker areas. If science is not your child's strong suit, your child should not sign up for the SAT II in Chemistry or Biology.

If your child declares a major on her application, make sure that your child has taken the SAT II subject test that is part of that area of study AND done well in it. Remember, an aspiring History major needs to prove that she will excel in her college-level history courses. A strong score on the United States SAT II or World History SAT II would demonstrate a solid foundation for college success as a History major. Aspiring STEM (Science, Technology, Engineering, and Math) students must consider taking the SAT II's in Chemistry, Physics, Biology, and Math (Level 1 or 2).

6. SAT II Language Tests

Your child should also take the SAT II in the foreign language she has studied in high school, and, if offered, in her native tongue. The SAT II can be used to test out of entry-level language classes once your child arrives at college and will allow her to complete her college foreign language requirement much quicker. Your child should take the SAT II in the language she is studying in her last year of that language study. If your child is not planning to take Spanish in her senior year, she should take the Spanish SAT II in either May or June of her junior year. If your child will take Spanish during her senior year of high school, she should take the SAT II in either September or October of her senior year. The more classroom instruction in the foreign language, the more prepared your child will be for the SAT II.

The College Board offers several SAT II language tests either with or without a listening component. What is the difference between the listening and non-listening tests? The listening tests are only offered in November, while the non-listening tests are offered at all other testing dates. Both tests ask 85 multiple-choice questions in sixty minutes. The breakdown of the non-listening test is 33% vocabulary and structure; 33% paragraph completion; and 33% reading comprehension. The listening test consists of a 20 minute listening component worth 40% of the score (e.g. describing a picture, continuing a short conversation, or answering comprehension questions); and a 40-minute reading component worth 60% of the score (vocabulary and structure, paragraph completion, and reading comprehension).

Before deciding to take a language test with or without listening, find out if your child's foreign language classes included exams that tested listening comprehension. If your child's listening abilities have not been tested, the pressure and novelty of the listening component in the SAT II may negatively impact your child's score. The decision to take one form of the test over the other is a matter of personal preference. If your child decides to take a language test with a listening component, she will need to bring an approved portable CD player and headphones to the testing site. Your child can also take both types of foreign language test, and use her higher score for her application.

IV. How to Set Your Child Apart from Other Applicants with the SAT or ACT

SAT or ACT scores alone will not make your child stand out. Even if your child aces the ACT, there will be plenty of applicants with perfect scores. However, you can ensure your child is a competitive applicant by ensuring that she is in the top bracket of applicants with respect to her entrance exam scores. As previously mentioned, Claremont McKenna had an 11 % acceptance rate in 2014, and 25% of the applicant pool scored a 750 or higher on the critical reading section of the SAT I. Your child should be among the top 25% percent of applicants with respect to the SAT I Critical Reading component (and the other components too) to have the best chance of gaining admission. The higher your child scores, the more competitive her application will be.

V. Conclusion

The SAT and ACT may seem daunting, but with planning that starts during the fall of your child's sophomore year, you can ensure your child has done the preparation to score the best she can. As a parent, your job is to set your child up for achieving the highest possible scores. By assessing your child's strengths and weaknesses through the PSAT and PLAN diagnostic tests and finding the appropriate test prep program, you will give your child the tools to obtain competitive scores for the colleges she will apply to and increase her odds of admission.

PART II:

Marketing Your Child As A Compelling Applicant Through The Subjective Application Components

Unlike your child's high-school transcript and entrance examination results that provide set grades and scores, the remaining parts of the college application are subjective and demonstrate value that is open to interpretation by admissions officers. No two college essays or sets of extracurricular activities are alike: your child can stand out by dazzling an admissions officer with perspective and maturity in her essays or with her commitment and leadership in her extracurricular activities. On the other hand, your child can rehash her accomplishments in her personal statement and blend in with the other tens of thousands of applicants by participating in a lot of activities but not leading or exceling in any of them.

Part II of *Earning Admission* discusses the subjective parts of the college application, including essays, extracurricular activities, responses to application form questions, letters of recommendation, and admission interviews. After college admissions officers evaluate applicants based on their academic performance and entrance examination scores, they will evaluate the subjective applications in their quest to construct a well-rounded and balanced class that will add value to their college.

With so much competition, your child must demonstrate her value to a college in the subjective application components. Each subjective component is an opportunity to persuade an admissions officer to admit your child. You must recognize that admissions officers look for certain traits and skills. Your child needs to highlight these skills and traits to increase her odds of earning admission.

Chapter 3:

Application Theme

I. A Theme Will Unify the Various Components of your Child's Application and Strengthen Her Application

Before we discuss the subjective components of your child's college application, let's discuss the important link that connects them and makes the overall application compelling: theme. Like a great movie or book, a theme can connect the different components and resonate with the intended audience—a college admissions officer.

Great movies' themes connect the movie with viewers. When I think of *Casablanca,* the theme of doing the right thing no matter what the cost comes to mind. In *Casablanca,* the main characters, played by Humphrey Bogart and Ingrid Berman, risk their lives to support the Allies as World War II rages. All of the characters' actions support the movie theme. The strong theme, which the plot develops and supports, is one of the (many) reasons why *Casablanca* is considered a masterpiece over 70 years after it was released.

Your child does not need to create the *Casablanca* of college applications. However, your child's college application will be more compelling if she is able to emulate *Casablanca's* excellent use of theme to unite the different parts of her application. The theme of a classic movie stays with us long after we forget the plot or the dialogue. Like an award-winning movie, your child's application will stand out from other applications if your child is able to develop a compelling theme.

II. What Admissions Officers Look for with a Theme: Added Value to College

There is no section on a college application that requires your child to state an application theme. Instead, an admissions officer will read the entire application, including the essays, extracurricular activities, letters of recommendation, and answers to form questions, and, if everything is cohesive, will remember your child's 'theme'. If an application is disjointed, or tries to focus on too much, an admissions officer will lose sight of the important parts and not identify its theme.

Certain themes are more appealing to certain audiences. *Casablanca* was released in January 1943 to tap into the patriotism and publicity associated with the Allied invasion of North Africa a few weeks earlier. Audiences connected with the theme of doing the right thing, no matter the cost, as the nation embarked on the necessary yet costly effort to liberate Europe and North Africa.

College admissions officers look for themes in applications that demonstrate an applicant's value. Value is the contribution an applicant is expected to make at the college she is applying to. Recruited athletes have little trouble showing the value they would add to a college's athletic department. In addition to adding value to a college's varsity sports team, an applicant can contribute to a university by joining its chorus or orchestra, being a leader of an organization or by contributing to a lab on research study on campus. An applicant can also add value to a college by bringing her perspective, maturity, and/or diverse life experience. Finally, an applicant can add value to a college by sharing her passion with other students and contributing to learning on campus.

III. What Your Child Should Do to Create a Compelling Theme

Compelling themes are built with every component of the college application—both the objective and subjective components. A successful theme unifies these components and makes them stronger. A college application theme is similar to putting a puzzle together. An individual piece may be pretty on its own, but slotted into place with the other pieces, a bigger and clearer image arises. To illustrate how your child can succeed at creating a compelling theme, let's look at two examples.

Example 1

Applicant A aspires to row crew in college. She is discussing joining the team with the college coach. Applicant A has applied to college as a Chemistry major. Her desire to study Chemistry is supported by 'A's' in AP Chemistry, Physics and Calculus AB. The summer prior to her senior year, Applicant A worked in a chemistry lab at a local university. Applicant A also scored very well on the SAT II Chemistry test. Applicant A has studied Spanish since 7th grade. She has a passion for Latin America. Applicant A tutors students who speak Spanish at home and volunteers to build schools in Mexico every summer through her youth group. Applicant A wrote her college essay on her first time in Mexico, and how it inspires her to become a chemist and conduct medical research to benefit emerging countries like Mexico tackle public health issues. Applicant A is a part of her high school honors society, but not overly involved in high school clubs or activities.

Theme: Renaissance woman; student-athlete; civic-minded future chemist. Whatever theme you take away from Applicant A's profile, it strongly demonstrates value to a college admissions officer. Applicant A plays a sport (even if not through her high school) that will contribute to her college's athletic program. Her personal statement ties her interests together and brings her passions to life. Applicant A demonstrates her passions and leadership by focusing on a few areas and making meaningful contributions in what she does. She would be expected to lead causes she cares about in college and continue her involvement in the community.

Example 2

Applicant B plays two varsity sports, soccer and softball, but is not competitive for recruitment for a national sports college. She hasn't thought of contacting a smaller liberal arts college like Middlebury or Colgate to see if she can play softball at either college. Applicant B is Treasurer of her senior class, President of two service clubs, and volunteers in her school's food drive every year. She is involved with several high school committees as well. Applicant B has a lot of academic interests. She does well in her classes. She enjoys English the most of all of her classes, so she has applied as an English major. Applicant B's entrance exams and high school transcript are competitive for the schools she wishes to attend. Applicant B's personal statement is about a challenge she faced as President of a club she is involved with because she is proud of being Club President and thinks it will impress the colleges she is applying to.

Theme: trying hard but not passionate; no theme detected. Applicant B may have the same grades and entrance exam scores, but her overall application is disjointed. Applicant B used her personal statement to rehash something she listed on her application, instead of expanding on it. Joining so many different organizations spread Applicant B very thin, and took away from her ability to demonstrate leadership and passion in a particular area that will be valuable to a college. Colleges have plenty of student members of organizations, but need the next generation of leaders to propel the student body forward. Applicant B would probably be involved in college, but maybe not focused on a particular area to create a legacy for herself and the college.

Takeaways

If Applicant A and Applicant B had the same SAT scores and identical high school transcripts, Applicant A stands out from the other applicants and has a much higher chance of being admitted than Applicant B. Applicant B will struggle to stand out among the other students with similar grades and entrance exam scores to gain admission. Applicant A used a theme to connect her interest, passions and skills to persuade an admissions officer she will add value to the college she is applying to. Applicant B did not tie the different parts of her application together. Her major choice is not supported by any other part of her application and her ability to contribute to the colleges she applies to is unclear. Applicant B made no effort to use her athletic abilities to gain admission to a college that may not be an athletic powerhouse, but still needs to recruit athletes for its teams.

This example illustrates why so many valedictorians and students with perfect SAT scores are not admitted to their dream colleges. The competition is too fierce to not tie the various components of a college application together to make them stronger as a whole. Your child must demonstrate she will add value to the college she wishes to attend. A compelling theme demonstrates high value to a college admissions officer. *Earning Admission* is written to prepare you and your child to create an application like Applicant A, not Applicant B.

IV. How to Set Your Child Apart with an Application Theme

College admissions officers will spend less than 15 minutes in their first review of your child's application. To an admissions officer, value consists of traits, skills, and activities that make up a well-rounded freshman class. Part II of *Earning Admission* will discuss the ways in which your child can demonstrate value, quickly, to an admissions officer in her application. As you read these chapters and formulate a plan for your child to build a compelling application theme, think of the following:

1. *Your child should emphasize desired skills, activities and experiences to create a compelling theme*

Not all activities create value for a college. Your child will stand out more for playing a sport that she can play for the college she applies to instead of playing three varsity sports that are oversaturated and face stiff recruitment competition. Make sure that your child emphasizes traits, skills, and qualities that admissions officers value in potential students.

2. *Quality not quantity*

Your child will be able to present the theme to her application by excelling in a few areas, and having deeper experience in those areas, as opposed to presenting countless activities and experiences that are less valuable or do not fit together.

3. *All of the application components must be consistent and enhance each other*

In the example above, Applicant A spent four years involved in the same tutoring project because it provided exposure to the Spanish language and Latin American culture. She wrote her essay about an experience she had volunteering in Mexico. Applicant A's personal statement demonstrated the perspective and maturity she gained on the world through volunteering. An admissions officer may not have appreciated Applicant A's interest in Latin America or understood the perspective she gained from her involvement in certain activities just from reading the activities she listed on her application; but Applicant A successfully showed her passions and maturity in her personal statement and therefore supported the theme of her application.

Like Applicant A, your child should use the different components of the application to build on each other and make the theme stronger. If your child applies to a college as a Chemistry major, she must have the coursework, SAT II scores, and demonstrated interest to prove she would add to that field in college. This will be discussed in greater detail in the following chapters; but, for example, your child could write her personal statement on why some aspect of chemistry, or its application, is important to her and her plans for college.

4. *Keep the theme simple*

Aspiring chemist-leader, civic activist-future doctor, scholar-athlete, all of these themes convey value to an admissions officer. The theme should be short, sweet, and focused. It is better to focus on skills, traits, or activities a college will value, as opposed to generic awards or non-leadership roles.

5. *Make sure that every part of the application supports your child's theme*

Your child will be busy growing and developing in high school. For the college application process, make sure that every part of your child's application works together to tell the theme.

V. Conclusion

Like a classic movie, a compelling theme in a college application will grab the attention of an admissions officer and help your child's application stand out from the rest. Your child will want to craft a compelling theme by demonstrating skills, traits, activities, and experiences that college admissions officers value.

Part II of *Earning Admission* discusses different opportunities for your child to demonstrate the value she can bring to a college campus. As you read Part II, think about how each different component ties together and demonstrates the value your child can offer.

Chapter 4:

The Personal Statement

I. Personal Statement: a Snapshot that Brings Your Child's Value to Life

The most important parts of your child's college application are numbers—her high school grade point average and entrance exam scores. However, with so many talented applicants vying for a small number of spots, the non-numerical parts of the application are the difference between acceptance and rejection. Your child's personal statement and any other required essays are a crucial opportunity for your child to stand out from the other applicants.

Your child must demonstrate what makes her valuable to a college in 500 words. 500 words is less than two double-spaced pages, and this word limit will require your child to be concise and focused. Your child will not write her autobiography, but instead offer a snapshot of what makes her compelling to an admissions officer.

The Common Application ("Common App"), a universal college application accepted by many colleges, offers five broad personal statement prompts (as of the 2015-16 application year). These prompts may change over time, but each one is open ended and designed to elicit responses that demonstrate the value an applicant would bring to the college. There is no 'right' essay for your child to write. If the essay does little more than recap some other part of your child's application, it will not add anything new to the application. The important part of the essay is not the topic, but how it portrays your child. Your child can write about anything as long as she ties her personal statement to the prompt. The five prompts are listed here, along with what an admissions officer is looking for:

2015-6 Common App Essay Prompts:

1. Some students have a background, identity, interest, or talent that is so meaningful they believe their application would be incomplete without it. If this sounds like you, then please share your story.

   - **Admissions officer**: show me why you are unique. I want to know why you are unique based on your perspective and the importance of your life experience to you, not just the skill or identity that you think makes you unique.

2. The lessons we take from failure can be fundamental to later success. Recount an incident or time when you experienced failure. How did it affect you, and what did you learn from the experience?

   - **Admissions officer**: I want to see your humility, perspective, development and what kind of person you are in the face of adversity. College is a challenge. I want to understand how you will persevere, not just what the challenge was.

3. Reflect on a time when you challenged a belief or idea. What prompted you to act? Would you make the same decision again?

   - **Admissions officer**: I want to see how you will disrupt the status quo. We want entrepreneurs and pioneers at my college. Show me how this experience has affected your perspective and growth and how it will affect your college career, not just what you did.

4. Describe a problem you've solved or a problem you'd like to solve. It can be an intellectual challenge, a research query, an ethical dilemma—anything that is of personal importance, no matter the scale. Explain its significance to you and what steps you took or could be taken to identify a solution.

    - **Admissions officer**: show me your passion or interest as it relates to solving a problem and why it matters to you and your college education. Passionate applicants make inspired and dedicated leaders. I want to know how your passion will impact your college career, not just what the passion is.

5. Discuss an accomplishment or event, formal or informal, which marked your transition from childhood to adulthood within your culture, community, or family.

    - **Admissions officer**: this is a trap—please do not write about winning a championship, or rehashing something you listed in your application and is common among the applicant pool. You are not unique for being National Honors Society President or just being involved with Habitat for Humanity. Describe something I would not know about from reading your application that demonstrates your perspective, maturity, and value to my college. Even if the experience is ordinary, demonstrate that your takeaway from it is extraordinary and will add to your college career.

Individual colleges often require supplemental applications, which may include another essay, usually shorter in length. A second essay prompt could ask why a student wants to attend a specific college, or ask an applicant to write about a meaningful accomplishment. Like the principal personal statement, any additional essays must demonstrate the value your child will bring to the college she is applying to.

II. What Admissions Officers Look for in a Personal Statement

1. *Ability to communicate.*

Your child will be tested in college. These tests will come in the form of essay questions and term papers. Writing will be a part of your child's college education. The personal statement is a way for a college admissions officer to assess whether your child can effectively communicate and handle the writing requirements of college. Admissions officers start with the basics: whether the personal statement responds to the prompt, demonstrates a strong command of English, displays style and substance, and, most importantly, whether it persuades an admissions officer that an applicant is valuable to a college. Admissions officers also focus on conventions. Your child has 500 words to persuade an admissions officer to admit her—ensure there are no typos within this short statement.

2. *Ability to follow directions.*

The Common App asks for 500-word responses. Your child must comply with this guideline. Even though the online Common App allows up to 650 words in the field for the personal statement, keep in mind how many applications each admissions officer must read, and you will appreciate the value of brevity.

3. *Focus.*

Your child will not have the space to write *War and Peace.* Admissions officers look for specific instances in an applicant's life, not autobiographies or recaps of an applicant's greatest accomplishments. By focusing on one specific instance, your child will have the room to expand on that instance's importance to her, which will enable her to showcase her perspective, maturity, and the value she will bring to college.

4. An applicant's unique attributes.

The personal statement is the only opportunity for your child to present herself in her own words. College admissions officers look for the attributes that make your child unique, compelling and valuable to that college beyond SAT scores and a high school transcript. Your child must demonstrate perspective, maturity, skill or passion to stand out from the tens of thousands of other applicants. Extolling the importance of being class president will not impress an admissions officer. There are plenty of other class presidents applying to the same college. Your child does not need to find the cure for cancer to come across as unique, but can focus on something that demonstrates authenticity and her own perspective on an event or issue. Make sure that your child's individuality and voice shine in her personal statement.

5. How an applicant will add value to the college.

Perspective: college admissions officers are tasked with selecting a well-rounded and diverse class. Diversity comes in many forms. If your child has had unique experiences growing up, or perspective gained from life experience that her application would not otherwise suggest, your child could use her personal statement to highlight these circumstances or experiences.

Maturity: your child may be as young as seventeen when she leaves for college in and not eligible to vote, but college admissions officers seek applicants with the maturity to take advantage of the opportunities afforded to them at a selective college. It is critical for your child to demonstrate that she will be able to lead the next class of students forward and meaningfully contribute to the university community.

Passions, interests, and skills: passionate and skilled applicants make dedicated and involved college students. Admissions officers look for applicants who will join the college orchestra, conduct research in labs, take part in competitive debate teams, and participate in other activities that make that college so vibrant. The personal statement is an opportunity for your child to demonstrate the importance a particular passion, interest or skill has for her that will also be valuable to a college.

III. What Your Child Should Do to Create a Compelling Personal Statement

1. *Start from the perspective of a college admissions officer.*

Your child must write an essay that demonstrates she will bring value to the college she is applying to, and portrays her as a compelling applicant. As parent, analyze whether your child's personal statement is compelling when providing feedback.

2. *Plan to write one spectacular personal statement.*

As your child narrows down the list of colleges she will apply to, compile the list of essay prompts required by those colleges. Check to see if there is overlap between colleges that do not use Common App and the schools that use the Common App for personal statement prompts. Your child should strive to write only one compelling personal statement. If there are different prompts your child must address for the colleges she plans to apply to, she should pick a topic that she can use for all of the colleges.

The personal statement should also be grammatically correct. With 500 words, there is no room for typos. You should proofread your child's final personal statement several times to ensure that there are no mistakes. Do not rely solely on support from your child's high school.

3. *Focus on a specific instance.*

Your child should focus on a particular instance that is meaningful to her, and serves as the means to tell a story that presents her as a compelling applicant. The instance can be anything, as long as your child expands on its significance to her and ties it to the value she will bring to college.

Your child has around 500 words to write a compelling personal statement. This makes the personal statement the equivalent of a snapshot into the mind of your child, not a movie. There is not enough room to rehash her life or greatest accomplishments. Summarizing an application adds nothing new to the application. Focusing on a specific instance allows your child to expand on its importance to her, which is far more important than the instance itself.

The same qualities that make a snapshot compelling, make a personal statement compelling. For a snapshot, the subject could be fascinating or the style and perspective may be unique. Other photographs convey the importance of the subject and are very powerful. An incredible snapshot incorporates all of these qualities. An incredible personal statement may have a unique, interesting or powerful combination of topic, style, perspective, and importance to the writer.

Admissions officers will caution applicants to avoid clichés. An ordinary topic without any unique perspective or significance to the writer could lead an applicant to blend in with the other applicants and not increase her chances of admission. It is okay to write about something cliché if it is important to your child. The instance itself is less important than what it means to your child.

An example is own personal statement. I wrote about the breakdown of my parents' marriage. This was the ultimate cliché. Based on the nation's divorce rate, half of the 244,000 Ivy League applicants could come from divorced families. I did not focus on my parents' pending divorce, but instead on the role reversal of having to be strong for my family to get through a difficult period and my transformation from child to adult. This instance was a defining moment for me and has shaped who I am. Two deans of admission from highly selective colleges referenced my essay, and the maturity and candor it showed, in emails and acceptance letters.

4. *Expand on the importance and meaning of the particular instance.*

The particular instance your child writes about is less important than your child's discussion of that instance's meaning and importance to her. Your child must convey *why* this instance is important to her and how it has changed her in a way that benefits the college she applies to.

Your child must also write about what she learned about from this instance. College is a learning experience. The personal statement shows what your child has learned in life so far and gives confidence to an admissions officer that your child will continue to learn and grow in the future.

The personal statement is also an opportunity for your child to showcase her maturity and perspective. College admissions officers look for students who have unique experiences and views on the world that will add to the learning environment of the other students.

5. *Tie the personal statement to college.*

Remember that an admissions officer evaluates your child's personal statement. It is not enough for your child to write an essay that just shows her growth or perspective. Your child must tie the instance and its importance to her college career and why she is valuable to a college admissions officer.

Connecting the personal statement to college, a proposed major or activity your child plans to continue in college, makes the admissions officer's job easy because your child will demonstrate the value she will bring to college. Think of the personal statement as an opportunity to provide an admissions officer a reason to admit your child.

6. *Your child's moment should also be the admissions officer's moment.*

The personal statement is about an instance that matters to your child. Your child should bring the admissions officer into this moment through effective writing. Your child should use a title that grabs the reader's attention and start the essay with a hook. Your child will want to engage the admissions officer from the beginning. If the essay is not interesting, your child runs the risk that the admissions officer glazes over and misses the parts where your child demonstrates the value she will bring to a college.

IV. Learning by Example: Effective and Ineffective Personal Statements

The following section provides three examples of personal statements. As you read them, put yourself in the position of an admissions officer. Analyze whether the essay demonstrated the student's value to the university he or she is applying to and whether it positioned the student as a compelling applicant. With personal statements, there is no need to reinvent the wheel. Your child should incorporate what works, and avoid what doesn't.

Example 1:

A Call to Arms

My heart beat fast as I realized that this was the end. Then it hit me. *Races condemned to one hundred years of solitude did not have a second opportunity on earth.* In that exact moment, Macondo, the surreal setting of One Hundred Years of Solitude, and Gabriel Garcia Marquez's symbol for Latin America, is wiped from the memory of man just as its remaining inhabitant realizes his fate. For Marquez, Latin America's failure to learn from its past mistakes, rejection of science and technology, and unbridled corruption proved fatal. His masterpiece is a warning cry, and a call to arms.

Growing up in sight of the US-Mexican border, the other side always captivated me. When I was young, the stories of gangs and fights seemed like something out of an action movie. As I grew older, and started making more frequent trips to Mexico with my parents, I began to notice the poverty and despair as soon as we crossed the border. I struggled with the stark contrast between the two sides: manicured green lawns, high-end outlet malls, and orderly business parks on the American side; shantytowns, public executions, and open warfare between federal police and *narcos* battling for control of the street on the Mexican side. I wondered what my life would be like if I was born just a few miles south from where I was.

When I reflect on my experience reading One Hundred Years of Solitude, I realized my heart was beating faster, not just because I was experiencing the death of a town and a people in a book, but also because I saw Macondo in my own backyard. Corruption and a raging drug war were leading many people to declare that Mexico was dying.

Latin America, with all of its troubles, is not dead. The region's potential is incredible and part of the reason I want to be an engineer. There is so much that needs to be built or improved in the world, especially in Latin America. When I am in Mexico, I experience failing utilities that I want to improve and drive on roads that I want to widen.

I hope to be a part of a story in Mexico that has a different ending from Macondo. Majoring in Engineering and Spanish will be my answer to Marquez's call to arms. By continuing my Spanish studies, spending part of my college career studying abroad in the region, and becoming fluent in Spanish, I will be in a position to contribute to the region's rebirth and growth. It is a tall order, but the challenges I will face in the next four years will serve as my foundation as an engineer and as an answer to Marquez.

Marquez may be right; races condemned to solitude do not have a second opportunity on earth. I do not think this applies to Mexico. Not now, for Mexico is not alone. I, along with many foreigners investing in Mexico's future, stand with it.

(Word count: 498)

Analysis:

1. **Attention-grabbing introduction**: title and the first paragraph draw the reader in. I want to know where this personal statement is going.

2. **Targeted subject matter**: applicant wrote about one of the most celebrated books of all time. This is great given the audience (an academic institution). It also shows how well rounded the applicant is. The applicant is an aspiring engineer who wrote an essay about wanting to become an engineer through reading a Nobel Prize-winning book. This essay establishes a strong theme that connects and enhances the other parts of the college application.

3. **Conveys a unique perspective** about growing up in a bi-national setting and the importance of this experience to the applicant and his plans for his college career. The applicant grew up in a unique environment—on the border. Just stating that the applicant is from San Diego on the application does not bring the applicant to life in as robust a way as the personal statement does. Ordinary experiences can lead to extraordinary perspective.

4. The personal statement **demonstrates significant value and potential** to a college admissions officer. The applicant shows the reader his passion for Latin America and how he plans to take advantage of academic opportunities in college. An admissions officer can see where the applicant will fit in at her university based on the interests and passion conveyed through the personal statement.

This is an effective essay that focuses on one specific instance, demonstrates the importance and meaning of this instance to the applicant, and demonstrates significant value to an admissions officer. The applicant scores brownie points for discussing a celebrated classic, grabbing the reader's attention, and demonstrating his plans for college and how well rounded he is.

Example 2:

<u>Twenty Years and Counting...</u>

When I was young, I wanted to surprise my Mom, so I tiptoed quietly behind her and gave her as big a hug as I could. I really surprised her— my Mom became stiff as a board as she tensed up. As I grew older, I continued to do this and elicited the same reaction every time. I began to realize that maybe the hug was doing something more than surprising her. My dad never tensed up when I gave him a hug from behind. He would laugh as he turned around. By the time I entered high school, I was over 6'3 and 200 pounds. The element of surprise was not my strong suit but, with every hug, my Mom continued to tense up. So I stopped giving her hugs altogether.

During my sophomore year of high school, I asked my mom why she didn't like hugs. I saw the look of pain in her eyes as she told me, "It's not *you* when you hug me, it's just that your grandfather used to come from behind and hit me." My jaw dropped as my Mom described the years of abuse she suffered at the hands of her parents. It took a while for me to get over this revelation, but accepting my mom's own pain led to a much more challenging realization: twenty years after my mom survived this abuse, she still was struggling with the pain.

Even though I was not old enough to apply for a driver's license, I felt the change in our relationship. My mom, the person our family was built around, who had protected my brother and I since we were born, needed help. It was now my turn to help her. I wanted to help not just her, but others who were in pain like my mom. I availed myself to listen to my Mom. I also started to volunteer at a domestic violence shelter. I wanted to support those fleeing violence and honor my mom's own survival.

My desire to understand why people struggle for years after experiencing trauma has led to my interest in psychology. I love studying the human mind and how it works. I know the more I learn about the human mind, the more I will be able to help my Mom and other survivors identify, address, and overcome their scars from abuse.

I am thrilled with the opportunity to continue my studies and be a part of the effort to learn more about the way our minds work. I also look forward to continuing to help my Mom and other survivors as a supportive friend or family member, as an advocate to prevent abuse, and as a student set on learning how best to deal with trauma after it occurs. As much as I would love to go back in time and protect my Mom, her strength inspires me to learn and help others.

(Word count: 496)

Analysis:

1. **Attention grabbing hook and introduction**: immediately grabs the reader's attention. I am interested to see where this essay is going from the beginning.

2. Personal statement **focuses on one specific instance**: applicant's mom revealing to him a history of domestic violence.

3. **Demonstrates unique life experience and perspective**: applicant is able to explain why this moment is significant to him and brings to life a unique perspective that an admissions officer would not have known about him.

4. **Expands on applicant's extracurricular activities and passions**: provides significance and meaning to volunteer activities listed elsewhere in the application. This essay adds to the application and makes it stronger by explaining the importance of one of the applicant's activities and why it is important to him and to the colleges he will apply to.

5. **Strengthens application theme**: psychology researcher, advocate, and compassion. The personal statement ties together the application components and brings the applicant to life.

6. **Demonstrates value to an admissions officer**: applicant connects the significance of the instance to what he wants to study in college. Applicant advertises himself as a future advocate and researcher in a lab on campus.

7. **Humanizes the applicant**: applicant shares a very personal moment and includes some humor about the applicant's size and ability to surprise. Applicant comes off genuine, sincere and caring. Applicant will stand out from other applicants bragging about their accomplishments in a shallow way.

This was an effective essay. It shows the applicant as caring and passionate and brings him to life from a psychology major on an application. The personal statement focuses on one particular instance that was very important to him, and expands on its significance both to him and his plans for his college education. The essay demonstrates value to an admissions officer through his passion (advocating for victims of domestic violence), interest (psychological research), and unique life experience and perspective (revelation of domestic violence and emotionally supporting his mother at a young age).

Example 3:

<u>We All Will Return in Peace</u>

It was hard not to notice the stares. Men, women, and children all look intently at me. I realized that my blond hair was peaking through my hijab, and my fair complexion and blue eyes stood out in a sea of black burqas. Just a day earlier, I had left my neighborhood in California, where every third home was exactly the same, and the people living in these identical cookie-cutter homes blended in with similar cars, clothes, and weekend activities. Today, I am in a different world in Abu Dhabi, and I am doing everything but blending into my surroundings.

My aunt sensed my trepidation as we entered an opulent home of one of her friends. Like me, she too has blond hair, blue eyes, and fair skin. Having married an Emeriti years ago, she has adapted to her country of residence far better than I have. "Don't worry, my dear, you have far more in common with the people here than you think."

She was right. As we were ushered into a salon with silk tapestries hanging from the walls, and a tea set made of gold in the center of the room, the stares I received on the street were replaced with smiling welcomes, hugs, and kisses on the cheek. Out of the presence of men, the black burqas were set aside and revealed colorful blouses, stylish jeans, and painted toenails. I admit I was surprised; some of the woman had dyed their hair blond. My aunt was right; I had more in common with these women than I thought.

Our similarities did not end with shared hair color. We spent the afternoon laughing about similar experiences travelling abroad, going to high school, and a desire to live in Paris one day. By the end of an afternoon filled with laughter, pitted dates, and Arabic coffee, I felt as if I had known these women for my entire life. My upbringing in liberal California with a 'reformed hippie' of a mother could not have been any more different from these ladies who grew up and live in a religious society where life is highly regulated and at times restricted.

As I left the afternoon tea party, the Emeriti women kissed me on both cheeks and implored me to return to visit one day. The farewell, "return in peace," stuck with me. We all hope to return one day to fond memories. In the wake of so much violence around the world, the wish for peace solidified our common humanity.

As a blond hair, blue-eyed California girl in the United Arab Emirates, I learned how to find our shared common humanity with people completely different from me. I believe college is about growing with others that are different from me and finding what makes us all human. I look forward to learning from others with completely different backgrounds than mine so we all may return in peace.

(Word Count: 494)

Analysis:

1. **Attention grabbing introduction**: good use of title and hook. I want to know why people are staring at the applicant.

2. **Cliché topic**: travel to foreign countries is not unique, especially the United Arab Emirates. Even if the applicant went to the North Pole, she must discuss the significance of the trip.

3. The **perspective** the applicant gained **is unconvincing**. The essay focuses more on the instances and less on the importance of the instance to the applicant. There is a baseline assumption we are all human. Just pointing that out is not enough. An attempt at humor with sandals underscores how little perspective the applicant gained from this experience. The repeated use of blond hair and blue eyes to demonstrate that she understands what it means to be different falls flat in *this country*. Compare the applicant's claimed understanding to the first essay. In Example 1, the applicant witnesses poverty and ties that to his inspiration to become an engineer. Here the applicant went to some type of a villa/castle/compound and observed trappings of wealth. The applicant tries to come off as worldly, but seems entitled and materialistic. Remember the audience and the purpose of this essay.

4. Applicant **fails to demonstrate value** from the experience or perspective to a college admissions officer. Applicant only writes about a vague interest in learning from others. Had she been captivated by her trip, perhaps she would want to study Arabic to contribute and grow in a more concrete way.

This essay started strong, but focused on a cliché topic (travel), and failed to demonstrate the significance of the instance to the applicant, or the value this experience would create from an admissions officer's point of view. The essay actually harms the applicant as she comes off materialistic and shallow. The applicant would be better served by focusing on what this experience meant to her and how that meaning ties to her college plans.

Example 3 is very similar to what my neighbor wrote for her personal statement. She was incredibly down to earth, sincere, and curious about the world. However, the essay focused on her experience being 'blond' in Abu Dhabi and failed to show who she really was and what was important to her. My neighbor and I had similar GPA's, test scores, and extra curricular activities. Three or four generations of her family had attended a prestigious Ivy League college (read: legacy points), whereas the only college graduate in my entire family was my father, who went to the University of Arizona. I outperformed her at almost every college we both applied to. The personal statement matters for a college application. A lot.

V. Strategies for College-Specific Supplemental Essays

Many colleges that use the Common App also require a supplemental application with an additional essay. Like the main personal statement, any other required essays should also demonstrate value to a college admissions officer and provide compelling reasons to admit your child. Your child should incorporate the same elements she will use in her main personal statement in any supplemental essays. Supplemental essays could ask the following questions:

1. *Describe your proudest moment or accomplishment.*

This question is meant to elicit a response about an experience that is important to your child. Like the main personal statement, your child should focus on one particular instance, expand on the significance of this moment or accomplishment and demonstrate the value that your child's perspective on this moment or accomplishment would bring to the university. Avoid clichés, unless your child can demonstrate value to a college admissions officer through the perspective gained.

If possible, your child should write about a high value accomplishment that demonstrates value to a college admissions officer. Accomplishments in performing arts, skill-based activities (like speech or a student newspaper), or something your child accomplished as a leader of a service or interest organization will bring that part of your child's application to life and to the forefront of an admissions officer's attention.

2. *Why do you want to go to X school?*

Your child may apply to a college that receives over 50,000 applicants. The college may ask your child why she wants to attend this college. Colleges are ranked in part on their yield, which is the percentage of admitted students who accept the admission offer and enroll. Admissions officers have an incentive to admit applicants who will attend their college if admitted. The 'Why X School?' essay must demonstrate that your child will attend the college if admitted. Your child can make that statement in the essay if she wants. It is not binding, unless your child applies early decision to this college (discussed in Chapter 10).

The 'Why X School?' essay should convey that school is a good fit for your child AND that your child is a good fit for the college. Your child could reference a specific major, program, location of the college, and any other factors that make the college exciting to her. The more specifics your child can reference, the more compelling the essay will be. Your child should also connect his or her own interests and skills to what excited him about a particular college and demonstrate that she will bring value to a specific program, activity or field of study at that college.

VI. Conclusion

The personal statement and any other required essays are snapshots that bring your child to life for an admissions officer. If your child's personal statement demonstrates unique insight, perspective, or life experience, her application will stand out and your child will have a better chance of earning admission.

Any essay your child writes must demonstrate the value she will bring to college to provide a compelling reason to admit her. By focusing on a specific instance, discussing the importance of that instance to your child, and connecting the importance of that instance to her plans for college, your child will be able to convey that she will add value to the college.

Chapter 5:

Extracurricular Activities

I. Extracurricular Activities: Focus on Activities that are Valuable to an Admissions Officer

Your child's achievements in extracurricular activities can distinguish her from the thousands of other applicants. College admissions officers value certain activities more than others. To increase your child's odds of gaining admission, she can pursue and excel in activities that will make her a coveted applicant.

Your child's extracurricular activities should support her application theme. For example, if your child intends to apply as a psychology major, she could dedicate herself to extracurricular activities related to psychology that demonstrate her passion for the field. Your child could serve as the student leader of a service organization that provides counseling to patients at a local hospital during the school year and participate in a summer internship at a local university's psychology department. If your child plans to continue studying Spanish in college, she could combine her interest in psychology with an international program that focuses on psychological services or research in Latin America.

If two applicants apply to the same college, have the same SAT scores and high school grade point averages, an applicant that could join the university orchestra or play squash at the varsity level brings more value to a college than an applicant who was a part of numerous clubs and causes, but cannot demonstrate additional value to a specific college program. An applicant that demonstrates more value to a college admissions officer is more likely to be admitted over an applicant that demonstrates less value.

This Chapter of *Earning Admission* focuses on crafting and marketing a compelling slate of extracurricular activities that will make your child stand out among the thousands of applicants Your child will use her extracurricular activities to demonstrate her skills, interests, and passions. By encouraging your child to excel in activities that college admissions officers covet, you will make your child a desirable applicant and help secure her a spot in the freshman class.

II. What Admissions Officers Look for with Extracurricular Activities

College admissions officers assess the impact an applicant's skills, passions and interests will make on a college. High-achieving students will play on college sports teams, be a part of programs like the orchestra and debate team, lead student organizations like the student newspaper or community service outreach programs, conduct research in a lab, and start new organizations and companies when they are not in class. College admissions officers look for the next class of students who will lead their classmates and propel the college forward. Your child can demonstrate value through her achievements in extracurricular activities. The more value your child brings to a college's programs, the more desirable your child will be to an admissions officer. When evaluating the value of an applicant's extracurricular activities, admissions officer assess:

1. *The impact your child could make at the college.*

The more skilled your child is at a sport, art form, or other activity, the more value your child presents to an admissions officer. The more valuable your child is in an activity that the college prioritizes, the more likely your child will be admitted to that college. There are a variety of college programs where your child's potential contribution could earn her admission:

a. **Athletics**: each year, varsity coaches and athletic directors recruit incoming freshmen to replace graduating seniors. Varsity teams receive numerous spots in an incoming freshman class.

Coaches for all varsity sports recruit athletes for their teams, not just the most popular or high profile sports like football or soccer. Even non-powerhouse colleges must recruit athletes. While Middlebury may not be competitive with Stanford when it comes to basketball, it still recruits student athletes for its team.

b. **Performing arts programs**: like athletic programs, college-sponsored orchestras, choirs and other performing arts institutions recruit new students to replace graduating members. Applicants that demonstrate an ability to contribute to a college's music and performing arts organizations will add value to that college and have a higher chance of gaining admission.

c. **Skill-based extracurricular activities**: college programs like the debate team and daily student newspaper also replenish their ranks each year. Demonstrating advanced skills and accomplishments in a skill that would benefit an official college extracurricular activity would also increase an applicant's value.

d. **Academic research**: an applicant who has already demonstrated an interest and/or impact in academic research through summer internships or independent research will demonstrate value to a college's research programs.

e. **Community involvement**: college admissions officers at selective colleges recognize the privileged position their students occupy with incredible resources and opportunities as part of their education. Admissions officers value applicants that have demonstrated a commitment to serving their communities. Admissions officers look for applicants that will be part of a college's efforts to serve and advance society.

f. **Unique passions**: unique interests and skills like robotics, computer programming or fluency in a foreign language stand out from other applicants' extracurricular activities and skills. Unique passions and skills are coveted for highly specialized college programs that rely on student participation. A college admissions officer will find an applicant highly valuable if she excels in a rare or unique field that the college offers a program in.

g. **International exposure**: a college education is designed to prepare students to thrive in international settings. Many colleges require students to demonstrate proficiency in a foreign language as a graduation requirement. Applicants who demonstrate international exposure and foreign language skills will add to a college's efforts to create world citizens in their students.

2. *If an applicant is a <u>leader</u>.*

Your child can also demonstrate immense value by showing, through her extracurricular activities, that she is a leader. College admissions officers look for students who will continue to lead organizations on campus, dedicate themselves to causes, and work to propel their classmates and college forward. Occupying a leadership position within a student or community position demonstrates a student's leadership potential.

3. *If an applicant is <u>well rounded</u>.*

Students with a variety of skills and interests draw on these to excel in their courses, and in their careers after graduating. Admissions officers seek applicants with a wide base of skills and interests that will propel them forward in their college and professional careers.

4. *What an applicant <u>achieved</u>.*

Admissions officers look for signaling devices that demonstrates an applicant's skill or achievement with an activity. For the performing arts, awards or acceptances for prestigious shows or performances signal achievement. For athletics, local, regional, or national rankings demonstrate skill. The more skill or achievement in an activity, the more valuable it is to an admissions officer.

III. What Your Child Should Do to Create a Compelling Profile of Extracurricular Activities

1. *Focus on passion and quality, not quantity.*

The value of your child's extracurricular activities is based on quality not quantity. An applicant that excels in a few areas will present more value with respect to those college programs than an applicant who is spread too thin. You should encourage your child to focus on activities and that she is passionate about AND excels at. The more passionate and interested in the activity, the more likely your child will excel at it. The saying 'quality not quantity' should govern what activities your child is involved with in high school.

2. *Keep track of your child's accomplishments.*

Your child should keep a notebook and record each activity she participates in during high school along with the time she spends each month on that activity and any of her accomplishments in that activity. The Common App requires your child to list extracurricular activities and the time spent on them. Recording your child's activities and accomplishments will make filling out the application easier, and ensure that any high value achievements make it into your child's application.

3. *Reinforce the theme through extracurricular activities that complement each other.*

Your child has countless options for how she spends her time outside of the classroom in high school. It is important to focus on activities that your child is passionate about and that fit together. For example, if your child is interested in studying psychology in college and intends to apply as a psychology major, she should pursue an internship or research program at a local university that focuses on psychology. In addition to pursuing research, your child could serve as a student board member for an organization that provides counseling services, and volunteer in a community service project that provides psychological therapies to veterans or homeless people.

The more your child's extracurricular activities fit together, the more clear your child's applicant theme will be to an admissions officer. By focusing on a particular area for service and leadership, your student will demonstrate interest, skills, and passion that will translate into your child being viewed as a student leader and therefore valuable to that college.

Your child does not need to join every activity. She will not have the time to lead or gain meaningful experience if she is overextended. Your child will be a more competitive applicant if she dedicates herself to a few activities as a leader and can discuss meaningful accomplishments within these areas.

4. *Use extracurricular activities to gain admission.*

We will now explore each type of extracurricular activity and how your child can use it to gain admission to the college of her choice.

A. Sports.

Be proactive: do not expect a college coach to contact your child. Your child must be her own advocate by contacting the coaches at the college she wishes to attend and play for. Discuss with your child's high school or club coach at what level, and at what types of colleges, your child could be a candidate. Your child should also research her skill level at a sport and what type of college she could compete for. There is no downside to trying to get your child recruited to a selective college through a sport. Keep in mind your child will demonstrate more value to a college if she also has competitive grades and SAT scores. There is a floor for a prospective athlete's grades and test scores, even for recruited athletes at selective colleges. The better the athlete's grades and test scores, the easier it will be for a coach to advocate on her behalf. High school students are allowed to contact potential coaches. Communication rules vary depending on the sports division, so your child should research when she can contact a potential coach.

Be open-minded with the college: some Ivy League colleges are national champs for certain sports and are at the opposite end of the spectrum for others. Many elite liberal arts colleges maintain substantial athletic programs as well but do not receive the same interest from student athletes since they are NCAA Division II teams. Highly selective colleges with varsity teams that are not national contenders still recruit athletes, and your child may be a valuable addition to that college's team. If your child is more interested in the academic caliber of the college she attends instead of the caliber of team, she should consider a selective college with a less competitive team. Finding the right fit requires research into the caliber of the college's team.

Widely-played sports (i.e. soccer, football, basketball, softball/ baseball): if your child is a high-achieving athlete in a widely-played sport but not a budding college champion or professional, consider smaller, non-powerhouse colleges. Ivy League colleges may not be frequent NCAA champions for sports like basketball or soccer, but they all boast fully-fledged athletic departments and take their Ivy League rivalry seriously. Other highly selective liberal arts colleges with smaller student bodies, like Middlebury and Williams, have football, basketball and soccer teams that your child may be a stronger recruit for than Stanford or Duke. If your child excels in a widely-played sport, cast a wide net and consider smaller, highly selective colleges that are not known for their team in that sport.

Consider less-played sports (i.e. crew or squash): some sports like soccer are played nationwide and boast hundreds of thousands of junior players. These sports are more competitive to secure spots on college teams. Other sports may be regional or do not exist within high school athletic departments. Many highly selective colleges have teams in these less-played sports and recruit athletes to join their teams. If your child is not a budding soccer, baseball, or softball star, consider taking advantage of the law of supply and demand by enrolling your child in a less-played sport like squash or crew. Crew skills can be developed relatively quickly, even if your child is already in high school. If your child starts crew in her freshman year of high school, she could be a potential college recruit by the time she applies to college. Many people in the country are unfamiliar with squash, especially on the West Coast (in case you are wondering what squash is, it is similar to racquetball). Like crew, many selective colleges have squash teams and, with less youth players, the competition for recruitment is less intense.

In short, less-played sports with less competition may open more recruitment doors for student athletes in the college application process.

Warm weather sports go further in the cold. High-achieving high school athletes seek to play warm weather sports in favorable climates that will allow them to play year round and develop their skills. For example, colleges like Stanford and the University of Texas attract some of the nation's top junior golfers. If your child plays a warm weather sport, consider colleges located in the cold. Colleges like Dartmouth, Middlebury, and Colgate (all near the frigid Canadian border) have *very* short golf seasons compared to Pomona College, which is close to Palm Springs. Consider contacting colleges with unfavorable weather for warm weather sports as the aspiring college champions and professional athletes will bypass them for colleges with locations that are more conducive to their athletic development.

B. Performing arts (choir, orchestra and other college-sponsored performing arts programs).

Like athletic programs, college performing arts programs must replace graduating members each year. Your child can demonstrate value to a college admissions officer if she can perform at the university level *and* add to a college's performing arts program.

Be proactive. It does not hurt to contact the director of a performing art program at a college your child is interested in attending and establishing a relationship that may boost your child's chances of admission.

Demonstrate your child's value to the program. If your child is an award-winning musician or a member of a prominent ballet academy, use parenthetical citations to list your child's accomplishments. For example: Member, National Junior Ballet Academy (lead ballerina in *The Nutcracker* and *Swan Lake*, performed in 6 states; won national ballet award for best junior lead performance 2015). Do not let a college admissions officer speculate as to the value your child will bring to a performing arts program at her college. Specify the accomplishments and demonstrate the value your child will bring.

C. Skill-based programs and activities (i.e. debate or student newspaper)

Demonstrate your child's value to a college's student newspaper, debate team, or other college-sponsored program. As with performing arts' accomplishments, use parenthetical citations to demonstrate your child's skill level and accomplishments with a particular activity. For example, Suburban High School Debate Team Captain (first place, San Diego High School Debate Competition May 2015; third place, California State Debate Championship September 2015).

Lead the organization when possible. Your child can increase her chances for admission by demonstrating leadership in skills-based activities. Your child should aim to become the captain of the debate team, editor of the school newspaper, or assume the leadership position in that particular niche. A leadership position shows passion for the activity and leadership. College admissions officers value both.

D. *Leading* a service, student, or interest organization

This section is not about being a member of a club or organization; this section is about *leading* them. The cardinal rule for being affiliated with an organization (student government, service clubs, interest groups, and community organizations) is: **there is no benefit from simply being a member in an organization. Your child must be a leader** to demonstrate passion, skill, interests, and *value* to a college admissions officer.

Demonstrate your child's value as a passionate and skilled future college student. For every activity listed, your child should cite examples (in parentheses). For example: Junior Class Vice President (led school food drive, raised 15,000 pounds of canned food for the San Diego Food Bank; organized 6 pep rallies for football games; planned Junior-

Senior prom with a $26,000 budget). Or: President and Founder of Milagros, a non-profit corporation (incorporated Milagros as a 501(c)(3) non-profit corporation; raised $6,500 from community sponsors, created a tutoring network for foster kids who do not speak English as a first language, oversaw over 1,000 hours of student-led tutoring from three local high schools). Unless your child explains her experience leading an organization, college admissions officers will not know the value your child can bring to their campuses.

Make sure that service and interest organizations support your child's application theme. If your child is interested in studying Spanish in college, then involvement in a community service organization dedicated to serving Spanish-speaking members in the community or Latin America would be consistent with your child's theme. If your child is interested in studying finance in college, she could start an organization that sponsors microfinance loans to entrepreneurs in Africa, or that works with the local Small Business Administration officer, for example. Whatever your child is interested in, reinforce her goals and application theme with leadership of an organization that fits with her goals.

Create the organization if it does not exist. If your child is passionate about a certain activity or cause, and there is not an existing relevant organization that your child can join, she could take the opportunity to start one and develop it. By starting an organization your child will demonstrate even initiative, leadership, and passion. When I was a junior in high school, I co-founded the Multi Culture Club. At my high school there were few community service-focused clubs. Most of my classmates in the club were studying Spanish so we focused on food and clothing drives for migrant workers that lived on the fringes of my community. Starting a service organization was critical for me to demonstrate my ability as a leader, commitment to serving the community, and reinforce my Spanish-speaking application theme.

Think Big. Just because your child is under the age of 18, does not mean that the organization she leads cannot make a significant impact. Your child could consider expanding the organization she founded and/ or leads to other local schools to create a network organization. Your child could also solicit corporate sponsorship or donations to expand the organization's reach; or incorporate the organization as a 501(c)(3) non-profit corporation. The more impact your child's leadership is able to demonstrate, the more value she will demonstrate to an admissions officer. The college application process is hyper competitive; your child has no option but to be grand to stand out.

E. Summer Internships

A summer internship at a local lab, university, medical practice, government agency, or other organization in an area of interest, would reinforce your child's application theme and demonstrate high potential value in that field as a college student.

Your child should be realistic about her role. She will be a high school student, not the lead researcher. However, if she contributes to the agency, project, organization, or research, she will be able to demonstrate her value to colleges.

If a formal internship program in your child's area of interest does not exist, consider working with a contact in an organization to create an internship opportunity. With a summer internship, the key is for your child to gain exposure to her field of study and gain experience in that area. Your child should list the internship along with a description of the organization's purpose and her role. For example: Psychology Intern, University of California, Irvine (assisted with intake interviews of research subjects; measured subject response to test stimuli). In English, this may mean that your child answered the door and counted each time a test subject blinked. Your child will have artistic license to market her involvement in a way that demonstrates value.

F. International Experience/Language Immersion

Your child could demonstrate a worldly perspective by partaking in an international experience during high school. An international internship coupled with language immersion would set your child apart and, at a personal level, be incredibly valuable to your child's development.

If you and your child are comfortable with the idea, your child could participate in some form of service mission or internship in a developing country. Your child could hit many birds with one stone by tying the experience to her intended major, working within a foreign culture and demonstrating commitment to community, *and* developing proficiency in a foreign language.

For example, if your child wants to study biology and later go to medical school, consider a program where your child can volunteer at a medical clinic in Mexico. Not only will your child strengthen her application theme of an aspiring pre-med student, but also she will add the theme of a world citizen and Spanish speaker to her application. Your child will also demonstrate that she has a global perspective and is committed to service, both of which are valuable to admissions officers. The experience will help your child stand out from other applicants through a unique life experience at an early age.

5. *Find opportunities for your child to demonstrate excellence in an extracurricular activity.*

You can find opportunities to demonstrate and showcase your child's skill and achievement in an extracurricular activity. Ranked athletes, artists who have displayed their work or performed at a prestigious event, debate champions—all have more credibility and demonstrate more value with respect to what they can contribute to a college.

Whatever your child's passion or skill, find opportunities for her to shine. If your child is a great poet, enter her in poetry contests. Keep track of the awards she wins, and make sure your child lists these achievements on her college application. Search for local, regional, and national awards programs (for all relevant accomplishments, including leadership of a community service organization, for example) for your child to enter, and, if she does well, this will give her the chance to stand out.

6. *Consider a summer program at one of your child's top-choice colleges.*

Some colleges offer summer programs for high school students, designed to either introduce them to college and/or offer high school class credit. Applicants who participate in these programs may develop stronger ties to that college that could help in the admissions process, though not every college offers a summer program for high school students. The programs could also be expensive.

If your child knows where she would like to apply before the summer of her senior year, you should contact the admissions office and research online to find out if there are any summer programs available at your child's top-choice colleges. If a program exists that does not interfere with any of your child's other commitments for the summer (SAT prep or activity consistent with your child's application theme) and the program is within your budget, you could consider the program for your child. These programs are not necessary, but, at the relevant time, something for you to consider.

IV. Conclusion

Extracurricular activities can demonstrate immense value to a college admissions officer. Applicants that can compete for a college's varsity athletic team, partake in a college-sponsored performing arts program, lead a student organization, or contribute to academic research, add value to a college and are, therefore, more likely to earn admission. Your child must excel in extracurricular activities to give her the edge among the thousands of applicants. By focusing on a few pursuits that your child is passionate about, your child will demonstrate skills and passions that admissions officers covet for their incoming classes—and increase her odds of admission.

Chapter 6:

Responses To Application Form Questions

I. Application Form Questions: Strategic Answers Can Strengthen Your Child's Theme and Appeal to Admissions Officers

The college application itself is a relatively straightforward process. Many colleges use **the Common App**. The Common App is what the name suggests: an online form that an applicant submits to any college that accepts it. On the Common App, applicants input their biographical information, their awards, classes, essays and extracurricular activities for admissions officers to review.

All of the Ivy League colleges and many highly selective private colleges including Stanford, Vanderbilt, and Rice, accept the Common App. Other colleges, including many public universities, do not accept the Common App. For example, the University of California has its own application for all of its campuses. Your child should use the Common App at any college she wishes to apply to that accepts it. The Common App will streamline the application process and avoid duplicative forms for your child to fill out.

Many colleges that accept the common application also require a **supplemental application** that is accessed through the Common App's website as well. Supplemental applications are usually shorter and ask your child to declare a major. It includes all the other questions that do not form part of the Common App (i.e. your child's favorite book).

This Chapter discusses how to use responses to form questions on the application to your child's advantage and how to respond to questions in a way that demonstrates additional value to admissions officers.

II. What Admissions Officers Look for in Responses to Application Form Questions

1. *No mistakes*

With so much competition, your child must not make any unforced errors with typos in the application. Typos suggest your child is careless, even though that may not be the case. You should proofread your child's application to make sure that it is grammatically correct.

2. *Comprehensive responses*

Your child will submit one application to each college. It must include everything that supports her theme and demonstrates that she is a compelling and highly valuable applicant.

3. *Diverse applicants for a well rounded class*

College admissions officers value diversity in their incoming class and attempt to create a well-rounded class with different perspectives, life experiences and backgrounds. Diverse and well-rounded backgrounds are more than an applicant's racial, ethnic, or religious identity. Admissions officers seek students interested in all of a college's programs, and take into consideration the gender balance of majors and schools within their college when selecting applicants for their incoming class.

III. What Your Child Should Do to Stand Out with Responses to Form Questions

1. *Strategic answers demonstrate an applicant's value to a college*

Every answer to a form question must support your child's application theme and portray your child in the most compelling manner to admissions officers.

Foreign language: admissions officers value foreign language proficiency. The Common App asks for your child to list the languages she is proficient in. If your child speaks another language other than English at home, OR has completed or is currently enrolled in an AP (or other college level) foreign language course, list those foreign languages in the application.

Test scores: your child should self-report only her best entrance examination scores. If your child took the SAT I twice, and will use a combination of the component scores, list both sets of test scores. Admissions officers evaluate your child's application with your child's best scores. There is no need to self-report everything; just give the best information requested within the application form.

Career plan: your child should select a career path that is consistent with her application theme. If your child is unsure about what she wants to do after college, she should still pick a career path that is consistent with her application (through demonstrated interests and experiences). Designating a career path on the application is not binding; admissions officers ask the question to better understand your child's passions and interests. The career path your child chooses should demonstrate a passion that will strengthen her overall application.

Submitting additional materials (i.e. art portfolio sample): admissions officers may allow applicants to submit additional materials that are helpful for evaluating your child's skill level in the arts or other field. Many colleges will state if they accept additional materials, the type of additional materials they accept, and the limits on these materials. If a college accepts additional materials, and submitting those additional materials could strengthen the application, your child should use this opportunity.

2. *Pick a major wisely*

Your child will select a major on her college application and should select one that supports her application theme. If your child has a strong, demonstrated interest in studying Psychology, Engineering, or Spanish, she should select that major on her application. Your child's major choice will reinforce her theme and add to the passion and interest she has displayed elsewhere in the application.

However, if your child's application theme focuses more on what she wants to do with her college degree (i.e. become a doctor, lawyer, or entrepreneur) rather than a specific course of study, your child should select a major on the application that (1) fits with that application theme AND (2) is a less competitive for admission.

Less selected major to stand out: college applicants select certain majors much more frequently than others. Choosing a widely selected major will not differentiate your child from the other applicants if it is not part of her application theme. Many applicants, who are interested in going to law school after college select Political Science or History majors in their college applications. Your child does not need to designate either major in the college application to go to law school and neither major supports a legal theme on their own.

If your child's application theme does not include a specific major or program, your child could pick a relatively unique major. Your child may be one of the few Brown University applicants that select Egyptology as her major, provided that some part of her application supports that choice. A unique major choice could differentiate your child from the other applicants and may provide a boost over an equally qualified applicant who is the 3,436[th] applicant that has declared English as her major. Your child can change her major later, as it is not usually a binding choice.

Less selective schools within a university: some colleges ask applicants to apply to a specific undergraduate school such as Liberal Arts, Business or Engineering. Some universities admit students specifically for the school they apply to, and therefore different schools within the same university can have different acceptance rates. Other colleges require applicants to apply to a specific school within their college but treat applicants at all of the schools the same for admissions purposes.

Before submitting an application to a university that requires your child to select a specific school as part of the application, you should contact the admissions office and ask if admission decisions are made for the particular school your child will apply to, or if admission decisions take into consideration the entire applicant pool across all undergraduate schools. If admission decisions are made on a school-specific basis, ask if they provide statistics on the different schools' admissions rates, and see which school offers the highest acceptance rates. Your child can then take into consideration the different admissions rates at each school.

Many colleges practice school-specific admissions. Cornell's Schools of Hotel Administration and Human Ecology provide a great foundation for students interested in business or science and have acceptance rates almost two times higher than in Cornell's other undergraduate schools. Historically, admissions for agriculture programs at California Polytechnic San Luis Obispo ('Cal Poly') have been significantly less competitive than those for business, engineering, and the liberal arts.

Depending on a college's policy on switching undergraduate schools, your child may be able to transfer from Liberal Arts to Business or from Engineering to Liberal Arts once she enrolls and begins her college career. Oftentimes, there is a GPA cutoff for transfers, but getting in and earning the necessary GPA to transfer is better than rejection and not having the ability to transfer. It is important to check with a college's internal transfer policies before your child applies. Sometimes transferring may not be possible or require a very high GPA.

I will provide an example from my own life. I applied to the College of Arts and Sciences at Penn. I had heard that it was twice as hard to earn admission to Wharton than as a liberal arts student at Penn. After one semester at Penn I decided that I wanted to study business. I took the necessary courses to be eligible to transfer and worked very hard to make sure my grades were above the GPA cutoff (3.70 for my year) to transfer into Wharton. I doubt I would have been accepted to Wharton out of high school.

Avoid competitive programs: applying to a less popular school or major within a university may significantly improve your child's odds for admission. Some schools are known for certain programs. Applicants interested in the Wharton, face more competition than applicants applying to Penn's School of Nursing or the College of Arts and Science. The same holds true with Northwestern's School of Journalism, which is considered one of the best in the country. If your child is set on studying Finance at Wharton or Journalism at Northwestern, she will have more competition for that program and will face lower odds of admission. Your child could apply to another program at either school, if consistent with her application theme, and potentially transfer or add a second major. Below is a list of a few highly selective colleges that have known differences in admission rates depending on the program.

Colleges with Varying Admissions Rates		
College	**Less Competitive Programs**	**More Competitive Programs**
University of Pennsylvania	Nursing (especially for men)	Wharton School of Business
Cornell University	Hotel Administration (29%) Human Ecology (25%)	School wide (14%)
University of Southern California		School of Cinematic Arts
Cal Poly, San Luis Obispo	Agriculture	
Northwestern University	Education & Social Policy	Journalism
Georgetown University	Georgetown College (liberal arts); Nursing and Health Science (especially for men)	McDonough School of Business; Walsh School of Foreign Service

3. *Address demographic factors if possible*

Earning Admission must address one factor that admissions officers take into consideration when evaluating an applicant: background. Background usually refers to an applicant's race. Affirmative action policies elicit strong responses from those who support and oppose them. I do not wander into the debate on the merits of affirmative action. Instead, *Earning Admission* offers ways to address college admissions officers' consideration of background when evaluating applicants.

Highlight any potential advantages your child may have. If your child identifies with a background that is underrepresented in higher education (Hispanic, African American, or Native American), she should identify as that. Since admissions officers try to select a well-rounded class from diverse backgrounds, identifying with an underrepresented group on a college application may provide additional value to an admissions officer and assist your child in gaining admission. If you are unsure of your or your child's background, it may help to do an affordable DNA study to see if your child has any links to underrepresented backgrounds in higher education that she can identify with.

If your child identifies with several different backgrounds, she should select any background that is underrepresented in higher education. Even if your child's heritage is just part Hispanic, African-American, or Native American, your child should identify with this background on her application.

College admissions officers also seek diverse and well-rounded classes for programs and majors as well. Your child could capitalize on gender imbalances within specific majors and schools. For example, there are more women studying nursing then men. In the eyes of an admissions officer, a male applicant would add additional diversity and perspective to a nursing program, and therefore would be valuable to the program. The same would be true for women applying for many science or engineering majors. Admissions officers would like engineering programs to be as balanced as possible between women and men. If your child's application theme supports selecting a major with a gender imbalance that benefits your child, selecting that major may help your child demonstrate diversity to that program, value to the college, and help earn admission.

Minimize any potential disadvantages your child may have. Your child may identify with an overrepresented group in higher education. Asian and Jewish students make up a far greater percentage of the student body at the most selective colleges in the United States than of the general population. If there are more Asian and Jewish applicants applying to the most selective universities, it may help to not self-identify with those groups. To an admissions officer, the more unique your child's perspective or life experience is, the more value she will bring to college. Your child should decline to state her background if she identifies with a group that is overrepresented on campus even if her name suggests an affiliation (read: Asian or Jewish if religion is asked).

I do not make the argument that a student's background can be harmful to her in the college application process. I identify with overrepresented population at selective colleges. I only suggest that applicants should position themselves as uniquely as possible since admissions officers place value on unique perspective when selecting students for incoming classes. Demonstrating unique perspective may be easier if the applicant does not self-identify with a group that is already a large presence on that college campus.

IV. Conclusion

Answers to application form questions are another opportunity for your child to strengthen her application theme and value to an admissions officer. By answering form questions strategically, your child will be able to demonstrate additional value by showing passion, interest, and perspective. Strategic responses to form questions such as major choice can also be used to demonstrate that your child brings a diverse or well-rounded background to a particular major, school, or to the student body as a whole.

Chapter 7:

Letters Of Recommendation

I. Letters of Recommendation: Additional Insight into your Child's Value

Many selective colleges require applicants to provide letters of recommendation from two high school teachers and an applicant's guidance (sometimes referred to as college) counselor. These letters of recommendation provide admissions officers with additional insight into your child's strengths and academic potential and are another opportunity to demonstrate your child's value, in the words of one education professional addressed to another.

The letters of recommendation are the only subjective part of the college application that your child will not write. However, your child can choose her recommenders and assist them in writing letters that demonstrate her value to an admissions officer. This Chapter discusses which teachers your child should ask, and what information she should provide her recommenders with, for writing strong letters of recommendation.

II. What Admissions Officers Look for in Letters of Recommendation

1. *Teacher recommendations*

Selective colleges typically ask applicants for letters of recommendation from two high school teachers. On the Common App, your child will designate her recommenders and input their contact information into the application. The Common App will then send the designated recommenders a form with instructions for writing and submitting the letter. Other schools that do not use the Common App have similar systems for recommenders or will provide your child with forms to give to her recommenders.

Admissions officers look for cues that describe the value your child will add to campus in the letters of recommendation. A letter of recommendation that provides additional insight into what your child is like in the classroom, and what makes your child unique from the perspective of the teachers, can help your child stand out from the other applicants. Admissions officer look for the following in teacher letters of recommendation:

A. What your child is like in the classroom

Admissions officers will know every grade your child earns in high school with her transcript. A letter of recommendation adds to your child's application if it discusses more than her performance in the classroom and sheds light on the type of student your child is. Is your child intellectually curious? Does she challenge herself? Is she passionate about the subject? Admissions officers want to know about your child's personality, her contribution to classroom discussion, ability to lead her classmates in learning, and her disposition in the classroom.

B. Your child's academic potential

Admissions officers want to understand your child's academic potential. Grades and SAT scores are considered the best indicators of an applicant's academic success in college. However, these indicators are not perfect. Admissions officers rely on letters of recommendation to gauge an applicant's *academic potential*. An aspiring engineer's application would benefit from her Calculus teacher describing her ability to grasp abstract concepts like differentiation. An aspiring Biology major's application would benefit from her Biology teacher describing her interest in the subject and how she competed in a local science competition.

2. *Counselor Recommendation*

In addition to letters of recommendation from two of your child's teachers, many selective colleges ask for a letter of recommendation from your child's guidance or college counselor. This letter of recommendation will also include a report on your child's high school that lists the advanced courses offered and the percentage of students that enroll in four-year colleges after graduating high school. Admissions officers look for the following from a counselor's letter of recommendation:

A. Your child's performance

Admissions officers want to understand if your child has challenged herself in high school. The information your child's guidance counselor provides allows admissions officers to assess the level of difficulty of your child's coursework relative to the classes offered at your child's high school. Every high school will offer different advance placement or honors courses. Your child must challenge herself with the courses she has available at her disposal AND earn as many 'A's' as possible in those courses. Admissions officers look to see if your child took advantage of academic opportunities available at her high school, and how your child performed in those classes.

B. Personal side of your child

Admissions officers also want to learn about your child's unique skills, interests, and passions from her recommenders as well. A letter of recommendation from your child's guidance counselor can discuss your child's involvement in school activities including sports, the arts, or leading an on or off-campus organization, and help put your child's accomplishments into the context of your child's school and community.

III. What Your Child Can Do to Stand Out with her Letters of Recommendation

Even though someone other than your child will write her letters of recommendation, your child can maximize the value these letters demonstrate on her behalf. Consider the following strategies:

1. *Your child should aim for strong letters of recommendation*

Your child should forge strong relationships with her teachers so they will be in a position to write quality letters of recommendation for her. Class clowns and cellphone addicts may not receive glowing letters on their behalf to demonstrate the value they will bring to a college campus. Your child should treat each class as an opportunity to prove that she is deserving of a quality letter of recommendation.

Your child, like me, may have little to no interaction with her guidance counselor outside of picking classes each year. Even if her interactions with her guidance counselor are limited, your child should treat these interactions with her guidance counselor seriously. Your child will want her counselor to hold her in high esteem when writing a letter of recommendation.

2. *Pick teachers in subjects that your child excelled in from sophomore or junior year*

Your child should ask teachers from her sophomore or junior year of high school to write letters on her behalf. Some high schools start in tenth grade, and college admission officers place more weight on an applicant's performance during tenth and eleventh grade, than ninth grade. Teachers that have only taught your child during twelfth grade have had less time to work with, and form a relationship with, your child, compared to teachers that have taught your child for a year or more. Recommenders will be writing letters as early as October for your child, which would give a twelfth grade teacher as little as two months to get to know your child.

The teachers who have taught your child for longer will be in a better position to write a comprehensive letter of recommendation.

Your child should approach teachers of classes that she excelled in (read: earned an 'A'). Your child will want her recommender to be able to discuss how well she did in the class. If your child hits it off with a teacher, she should ask that teacher for a letter of recommendation. The more positive the experience, the more the teacher will be able to discuss in the letter of recommendation

3. Pick teachers that are consistent with your child's application theme

Your child should ask for recommendations from teachers who taught them the subjects that are consistent with her application theme. The letters need to come from teachers that have taught your child the subject areas they would like to pursue in college, as these are the teachers who will be able to demonstrate your child's abilities in this area of study.

For example, an aspiring engineer should ask her tenth or eleventh grade math or science teachers for letters of recommendation. A recommendation from a math or science teacher will provide more meaningful insight into your child's academic potential in a field that is directly relevant to an engineering student's college studies. An additional letter of recommendation from the humanities (history, English, or foreign language) can demonstrate that an aspiring engineer is well rounded, but is insufficient on its own to demonstrate an aspiring engineer's potential for the bulk of her quantitative college coursework.

4. Consider building a relationship outside the class

Teachers that can draw on interactions with your child from outside the classroom will be able to write more insightful letters of recommendation about your child's personality and unique attributes. If your child has a favorite teacher from a subject consistent with her application theme, she should consider asking that teacher to be the faculty advisor for a service or interest organization that your child leads on campus. An additional opportunity to work with your child will provide a teacher with more material for writing a letter of recommendation, including your child's leadership abilities.

5. Give recommenders material they need to write an excellent letter of recommendation

The better prepared the recommender, the better the letter of recommendation. A recommender does not have to rely solely on her interaction with your child in the classroom for her letter. Your child should provide her recommenders with information about her passions, interests, and skills in and outside of the classroom, along with her college and career plans, so the teachers and counselor can write letters that tie in their experience of working with your child to your child's application theme.

Many high schools provide students with information forms to complete and give to their recommenders. Your child will be asked to list her interests, intended college major, and extracurricular activities. If your child's high school does not provide a standardized form, your child should draft a short memo that will assist her recommenders in writing a letter. Your child should include:

(1) The schools she is applying to;

(2) Intended college major;

(3) Why she wants to study that subject in college;

(4) Her extracurricular activities in high school and accomplishments in those activities; and

(5) Any information that demonstrates value to an admissions officer involving your child's unique skills, interests, passions, or life experience that a high school teacher could refer to. The more context your child's recommenders have, the more value they will be able to demonstrate on your child's behalf.

6. *Give recommenders sufficient time to write a quality letter of recommendation*

Your child's recommenders will need as much notice as possible to have sufficient time to write a quality recommendation. It is likely that they will have to write letters of recommendation for other students as well—on top of the lesson plans, grading, and meetings teachers and counselors must also attend to every day. Your child must recognize the tight deadlines teachers and counselors have for writing letters of recommendation and the limited time at their disposal.

Your child should ask her potential recommenders to write on her behalf as early as possible in senior year (read: no later than September). Early decision and early action applications and letters of recommendation are due as early as November 1st, with regular decision applications following shortly thereafter in early January. By asking her recommenders to write on her behalf in September, your child will ensure they have enough time to write quality letters. Your child should ask her recommenders what information they need, in addition to any forms the school requires; or whether the brief memo suggested above would be sufficient.

Your child should follow up with her recommenders to make sure that they submit their letters of recommendation by the deadline. My Spanish IV teacher, who I am still close with, did not realize that the deadline for my early decision letter of recommendation was earlier than my regular decision applications. By following up with my recommender, I was able to avoid a potential disaster. She submitted the letter of recommendation for my early decision application just a few days late instead of months late, and my application was complete in time for early decision review.

Finally, make sure your child thanks her recommenders with a small gift or thank you card. Her recommenders have advocated for your child to earn admission on their own time.

IV. Conclusion

Your child's letters of recommendation are another opportunity for your child to demonstrate the value she will bring to the college. Your child's teachers and guidance counselor will provide college admissions officers with insight into your child's academic potential and the type of student your child is. Your child should pick teachers in subject areas that are consistent with her application theme and that can discuss her academic potential in a subject that is relevant to her intended course of study.

Your child can assist her recommenders by providing them with information about her skills, passions, interests, and perspective. The more prepared your child's recommenders are, the more value their letters will demonstrate.

Chapter 8:

Admissions Interview

I. Admissions Interviews: They May Only Marginally Help Your Child, but Still Another Opportunity for Your Child to Demonstrate Value and Interest in a College

Many selective colleges offer an optional admissions interview as part of the application process. Interviews tend to be conducted by local alumni or, if you live in an area with few alumni, over the phone. A few colleges offer interviews with admissions staff as part of a campus visit or admissions officer tour. Because not all applicants are able to interview with alumni or an admissions officer, the interview is not given as much weight as the other application components.

The admissions interview may cause anxiety. However, your child should not worry. As not all applicants will be able to partake in an admissions interview, the interview cannot harm your child or any other applicant who is either uncomfortable during the interview or unable to interview. The interview should simply be viewed as another opportunity to demonstrate her value to a college and to learn about a college she may attend.

1. *Alumni Interviews*

The most common type of admissions interview is an alumni interview. An alumnus could be a recent graduate or someone who graduated from college thirty years ago. Colleges ask their alumni to interview to engage their alumni, not your child. The more engaged alumni are, the more likely they are to donate. There is minimal training and no quality control for alumni interview reports, so admissions officers do not give much credit to what alumni write about an applicant. Admissions officers recognize that alumni are not professional admissions officers and are not in a position to assess your child's value to the college. The process is intended to give your child an opportunity to hear about an alumnus' experiences at a college and for colleges to maintain constant interaction with their alumni.

There is great variance between alumni interviewers. Some engage applicants and have an enlightening discussion about their alma mater, while others use the interview as an opportunity to hear themselves talk for thirty minutes or an hour. Some alumni are able to write persuasively about why an applicant they interview would be a good fit for their alma mater and others cannot.

It is possible that if your child's interviewer writes an incredible interview report about her and she is competing for the last remaining spot with one other applicant who had a mediocre interview report, your child may edge out the other applicant. However, admissions officers will prioritize every other component of your child's application before relying on an alumni interview report to make an admissions decision.

2. *Admissions Staff Interviews*

Some colleges, including the University of Southern California, conduct admissions interviews with admissions officers either on campus or off campus. These colleges will not interview every applicant and therefore an applicant's interview performance or lack of an interview will not count against her. If your child applies to a college that offers admission officer interviews and it is possible for your child to participate, your child should take advantage of the opportunity to potentially meet with the person who will decide to admit your child.

Interviews may be secured on a first-come, first-serve basis, so it is important that your child finds out if any colleges she plans to apply to offer admission interviews with admissions officers, and that she signs up for a slot as soon as she can. Colleges may claim that interviewing with admissions officers will not make a difference to your child's odds of admission, but establishing a personal connection with an admissions officer will benefit your child in the admission process and demonstrate that your child is interested in attending that college.

II. What Admissions Officers Look for in an Admissions Interview

Both admissions officers and alumni will interview applicants and write a brief report on the interview that will be included in an applicant's application file. Even if an application interview report is not given much weight in the application process, your child should still take advantage of the opportunity to meet with an alumni or admissions officer and demonstrate interest in attending that college and the value your child would bring to it. Admissions officers look for the following in an interview report:

1. *Conforms with social norms*

Admissions officers will give your child the benefit of the doubt and assume she understands basic societal conventions, like not texting during an interview or bringing a parent to the interview, unless your child commits a major faux pas that an interviewer feels compelled to report. The interview is the only human interaction that is part of the admissions process. Your child must present herself in the best light possible and not come off as rude or immature.

2. *Interest in attending the college*

A college's yield, or rate that accepted students enroll at that college, is a factor in college rankings. College admissions officers have an incentive to admit students who will accept an admission offer. Your child **must** tell the interviewer that the school she is interviewing for is one of her top choices, and that she is highly likely to attend if accepted. Your child's remarks about attending a particular college are not binding, and the admissions competition is so fierce that she must provide admissions officers every reason to admit her that she can. Depending on your child's admission cycle, that particular college may become her top choice if she is admitted there. Your child should make admitting her easier for an admissions officer who is concerned about her college's yield.

3. *Reasons why your child wants to attend the college*

Your child should provide reasons that support her interest in attending that particular college—reasons that are credible and convincing. Your child should discuss the specifics of why she wants to attend that college and reference a specific major, program, extracurricular activity, location, or anything else about the college that is appealing to her. Your child should tie these reasons to her own skills, interests, passions and perspective, so she demonstrates her value to the college as well.

4. *The value your child brings to college*

Earning Admission has discussed at great length the importance of demonstrating value through skills, interests, passion, and perspective. The admissions interview can be viewed as another opportunity for your child to demonstrate the value she would bring to the college. Alumni interviewers are volunteers and look for reasons to advocate that your child should be accepted. While your child should not brag, she should give her interviewer reasons to advocate on her behalf.

III. How Your Child Can Stand Out in the Admissions Interview

1. *Do not bring Mom or Dad*

In a sign of the times, it is worth mentioning that parents should not be a part of the application interview, or any interview their child participates in, unless explicitly invited unilaterally by the interviewer. Your child cannot ask to bring you to the interview and then think it is okay to bring either parent. I had one interview where the interviewer wanted to meet my Mom as she picked me up from the interview. That is okay. However, if your child asks to bring you or brings you to the interview, she will appear as if she is unable to cut the cord for college the following year. If you or your child is anxious about the interview, wait outside the interview venue. Interviews are usually held in public places like Starbucks.

2. *Be professional*

Again, in a sign of the times, it is worth mentioning your child must treat the interview seriously and display courtesy and respect for the alumnus or admission officer interviewing her. HR managers frequently post online horror stories of distracted or rude millennials that text, interrupt, or leave in the middle of the interview. Your child's goal is to convince the interviewer to advocate on her behalf. Texting during the interview will create little goodwill between your child and the interviewer. Your child should make eye contact, smile, and talk confidently. This interview will be one of the first of many interviews in your child's life. It is excellent practice for future job interviews.

3. *Dress appropriately for the interview*

Your child should dress appropriately for the interview. The dress code may be specified if an interview is held in a structured format (i.e. all interviews for applicants for a college living in a city could be conducted at one high school or hotel conference room on a set day). If not, your child could ask the organizer what she recommends in terms of dress code. If you are unable to determine if a structured interview program has a dress code, your child should err on the side of caution and dress business-casual.

For the overwhelming majority of interviews that occur in informal settings, like a coffee shop, your child should take a cue from the interviewer when they invite her to meet. If the interviewer does not specify what to wear, your child should again err on the side of caution and dress in business-casual. Dressing professionally will demonstrate your child takes her application to that college seriously. If your child's interviewer tells her that the interview is casual and that she can wear jeans, she should do that yet look presentable (no rips, holes, or obscene material). Most alumni I know who conduct interviews tell applicants that jeans are okay for the interview. Even if the interview is casual, discourage your child from wearing athletic or loungewear. Your child will want to make a professional first impression even if the clothing is casual.

4. *Tell the interviewer that she wants to go to that college*

Your child will want her interviewer to report that she is likely to attend if admitted and help admissions officers protect their yields; so she needs to tell her interviewer that she is very likely to attend if accepted. As your child has applied for her preferred colleges, she is stating a fact when she says it is highly likely she will attend that particular college.

If an interviewer asks your child why she did not apply early decision to that college, she can tell the interviewer that she could not commit to attending a school without knowing the financial aid or scholarship package she would receive. If the interviewer asks why she did not apply early action to that college, your child could say her application was not ready by the early action deadline.

5. *Do not disclose applications to 'more prestigious colleges'*

Your child will be a more compelling applicant if the admission officer believes your child wants to attend her particular college above all others and, enhance that college's yield. Your child should not disclose if she has applied to a 'more prestigious college' in the interview process because this will discredit her claim that she wants to attend the college she is interviewing for. For example, an applicant interviewing for a selective, but non-Ivy League, college does not need to disclose that she also applied to Harvard. The applicant gains nothing by disclosing her application to Harvard and no admissions officer wants to feel that an applicant would rather enroll somewhere else. If your child applied early decision or early action to another college, she should not disclose this because it signifies that *that* college is your child's top choice.

6. *Provide specific reasons why your child wants to go to that college*

As colleges want to admit students that will enroll if accepted, an interviewer is likely to ask your child why she wants to attend the college she is interviewing for. Your child should be prepared to answer this question by referring to specific programs or characteristics of the college that interest her. For example, your child could refer to the freshman curriculum, the location of the college, or unique programs offered (academic, community, research, etc.) that interest her to the point your family has spent $75 to apply there. Your child may want to attend Duke because it is a great college, but she must provide a more specific answer when asked why she wants to go there.

Your child should tie the reasons she wants to attend the college to her own skills, passions, interests, and perspective. Like the response to the 'Why X School?' essay question, your child should treat the admissions interview as an opportunity for your child to demonstrate that she is a good fit for the college and the college is a good fit for her.

7. *Demonstrate value to the college*

Similar to personal statement prompts, colleges provide alumni interviewers with suggested questions that enable applicants to demonstrate their value to a college. Interviewers will receive little, if any, personal information about your child prior to the interview. Interviewers will ask broad questions to get to know your child and write their report.

Your child should discuss her skills, interests, passions, and experiences that would make her valuable to that college. If the interviewer asks your child about her involvement in extracurricular activities or accomplishments in high school, she can take the opportunity to highlight these in a way that would make admissions officers find her valuable to the incoming class.

Your child can demonstrate additional value by tying what she discusses to programs and activities at that college. For example, an aspiring biology student could discuss her summer internship at a science lab at a local university and expressly link this to her interest in conducting research in a biology lab in college.

8. *Engage the interviewer about her experience*

The interview is an opportunity to ask the interviewer about their experience at that college. For many alumni interviewers, the college experience was transformative. Your child may learn about a college program that could change her path. The interview should include as much learning about a college for your child as it does for an admissions officer or alumnus learning about your child's unique skills, interests and passions. Your child should take advantage of an opportunity to learn about that college from a person who experienced it.

Asking the interviewer to discuss her college experience will also take the pressure from your child to do all of the talking. Asking questions will also engage the interviewer. The more engaged the interviewer, the more likely it is that he or she will like your child and write a more favorable report.

IV. Conclusion

Even if the interview may only provide, at best, a marginal benefit to your child in the application process, it is still an opportunity for your child to stand out from other applicants and demonstrate her value to a college admissions officer, either directly or through an alumnus who writes a report for her application file. Your child should demonstrate a strong interest to attend the college and tie her passions, skills, and interests to the specific programs at that college. Interviews are also an excellent opportunity for your child to learn about that college from alumni.

PART III:

Application Strategy

Part I and Part II of *Earning Admission* discuss how to use each component of the college application to demonstrate value and persuade an admissions officer to admit your child. Part III of *Earning Admission* enhances your child's applications by discussing how to use strategy to select the 'right' colleges for your child to apply to. Furthermore, by keeping an open mind in selecting colleges that offer merit scholarships and/or need-based grants, your family may reduce your family's contribution for your child's college education by hundreds of thousands of dollars. Part III also discusses timing your child's applications to increase her odds of admission to her top choice colleges.

Finally, Part III discusses the strategy your child should use to earn admission from a college's waitlist. While being placed on a waitlist is not an ideal outcome for your child, it provides her with an additional opportunity to demonstrate value to an admissions officer and earn admission to that college.

Chapter 9:

Where And When To Apply

I. Where and When Your Child Applies Will Dictate Her Admissions Cycle

You and your child will work together to create a list of colleges your child will apply to, taking into consideration the fierce competition she will face, the cost of attending the different colleges, and her preferences, goals, and aspirations. Putting together a list of the 'right' colleges for your child is challenging given the competition for highly selective colleges and the cost of a college education. This Chapter discusses finding colleges that provide the experience your child wants, instead of focusing just on 'name-brand' colleges. This Chapter also offers suggestions for less conventional college choices that may be excellent fits for your child and offer higher admission rates.

The timing of your child's applications may also significantly improve her odds of admission. Some colleges offer rolling admissions, which means they either admit or deny applicants as the applications are received. The more slots available, the higher your child's odds of acceptance will be for that college. Furthermore, some colleges have much higher admission rates for early decision or early action application programs, which your child should capitalize on as well. This Chapter discusses the benefits of your child applying early to her top choice college(s).

II. Creating an Appropriate College List

1. Go on the offense with reach schools

Your child will likely apply to colleges that she would love to attend but, given the number of applicants those colleges receive, faces low odds of admission. These colleges are referred to as 'reach schools'. Even if your child implements all of the suggestions in *Earning Admission*, she may still not gain admission to some highly selective colleges. Some highly selective colleges are reach schools for all applicants. For example, in 2015, Brown University rejected 77% of applicants who scored a perfect 800 on the SAT I Math component.

There are other colleges that are highly selective and admit less than 25% of applicants as well. If your child does not have exceptional grades and entrance exam scores that place her in the top 25% of the applicant pool for those colleges, these colleges will be reach schools for your child. Your child can apply to these colleges, and if she demonstrates enough value elsewhere in her application, may gain admission. It has been done in the past, and your child can do it. However, you and your child should recognize that gaining admission to these colleges is a *reach*.

2. Play defense with safety schools

Selective colleges can fill an entire class with valedictorians and perfect SAT scores. Because there is no guarantee that your child will gain admission to her reach schools, your child will also need to apply to a few colleges where she is highly likely to gain admission, based on her grades and entrance examination scores. Your child must protect herself and earn admission to at least one college she would be content to attend.

It is less exciting coming up with contingency plans than figuring out how to earn admission to your child's dream college. While building a compelling profile for college admissions officers, your child could also consider applying to less selective flagship state universities. Your family may reap the savings of in-state tuition prices (read: a lot cheaper) and your child may have opportunities to be part of an honors program or honors college that provides personalized experiences and support for applying to graduate programs.

Your child should also consider secondary campuses for public state universities if the local flagship university (i.e. UC Berkeley or the University of Texas) is a reach school for all applicants due to the volume of applications they receive.

Finally, your child could also consider private universities that offer generous scholarship packages to applicants at the top of the applicant pool. If a private university costs the same or less than an in-state public university it may be great fit for your child if she is seeking a smaller and more intimate college environment.

3. Define and implement objective criteria for creating the college list

There are thousands of colleges that your child could apply to. Your family should develop criteria, based on your child's preferences and your family's ability and willingness to pay for certain colleges, to create a list.

For example, your child may decide that she wants to apply to colleges that (1) are located in suburban or rural settings with a college-town feel; (2) are on the East Coast or less than eight hours driving distance from her hometown in New Jersey; (3) offer mechanical engineering programs; and (4) offer a college-sponsored ballet program.

Taking into consideration your child's SAT scores and high school transcript, your family will assemble a list of colleges that include both reach and safety schools. A sample list could include Carnegie Mellon, Rutgers, Penn State, Lehigh, Franklin & Marshall, and Cornell.

Another applicant may want to attend a small liberal arts college to study biology in either the Northeast or Midwest. Factors the applicant could rely on are: (1) location; (2) small class size; (3) study abroad programs in Spain; (4) creative writing programs or workshops. This applicant, depending on her SAT scores and high school transcript, may assemble a list of colleges that includes Middlebury, Colgate, Williams, Haverford, Grinnell, and Kenyon.

By implementing objective criteria that focus on the experience your child wants in college, your child may identify colleges she did not previously consider that offer higher rates of admission. If your child just focuses on 'name-brand' colleges that she knew about before she applied, she might only apply to those that admit less than 15% of their applicants. Instead, by searching on experience, she can identify other colleges that may be a great fit for her *and* admit a higher percentage of applicants, which will provide her with higher odds of obtaining the college experience she wants.

4. Determine under what conditions your child would attend a higher-cost college

Before your child applies to college, you must discuss with her the conditions for your family to pay the difference to attend a higher-cost college. If paying for college is not an issue, your child may have few restrictions on the colleges she applies to. For the overwhelming majority of families (mine included), the cost of college is an issue and must be addressed before your child applies and not when you or your child receives the first loan repayment notice.

When creating your child's college list, consider your family's finances, potential scholarships and grants, and the ability or willingness of the student and/or family to take on loans to finance the college education. Some families are willing to make sacrifices for their child to attend a prestigious college like Harvard or Pomona College instead of an in-state public university, but would not pay the cost difference for a 'less prestigious' private university. You must ask yourself what colleges your family is willing to pay for and under what circumstances.

Before you tell your child she cannot apply to private colleges outside of the Ivy League, you should understand that the listed price to attend a college may not be the cost for your child. The next Chapter will discuss maximizing merit scholarships and need-based grants.

5. How many colleges should your child apply to?

Your child will need to apply to at least one or two 'safety schools'. Beyond that, it is a matter of your family's preferences and budget. Each college application can cost upwards of $70 including the application fee and required entrance exam score report. Many students apply to 10-12 colleges, with some applicants applying to as many as 20. Given the competition, you may be enticed to encourage your child to apply to many more colleges, but keep in mind that each college may have its own application or require a supplemental application to the Common App and that the costs and time required to apply to each college add up very quickly. There is no right number for college applications. I applied to 17 colleges and found the process to be overkill. I applied to too many safety schools and at least one reach school that I would not have attended. In hindsight, I would have applied only to colleges I would have attended.

Most colleges offer fee waivers for applicants with limited financial resources. Typically, an applicant that qualifies for free or reduced lunch programs in high school would qualify for a fee waiver. If this is something that may apply to your child, consult with the admissions offices of the colleges your child is interested in applying to in September of your child's senior year.

6. Should your family go on college visits?

It has become a rite of passage for high school students to visit prospective colleges during the spring break of their junior year of high school. College admissions offices offer student-led tours and information sessions with admissions officers to teach applicants about their colleges and the application process.

If the cost of the college search process is not an issue for your family, college visits are exciting, informative and a great way to see the country. However, if your family must prioritize college expenditures, it is better to invest in your child in ways that increase her odds of admission including SAT and class tutoring. Most colleges offer no admissions boost to students for visiting their campus prior to applying. Information sessions tend to cover information that is available online. Your child can use objective criteria to identify the type of colleges she applies to and then tour the colleges she has been accepted to.

I toured at least 20 campuses on two separate college tours to the East Coast during my junior year of high school. I should have saved my parents thousands of dollars by waiting to see where I was accepted and then visiting those colleges. I ended up choosing between the only two colleges I did not visit before I applied.

III. Be Open Minded to Gain Admission to Potential Great Fits for Your Child

1. Find colleges that offer similar experiences and admit more applicants

College is an experience. While certain colleges have more cache associated with their name, your child has the power to create the experience that she wants wherever she attends. Your child must be open minded when seeking colleges that are good fits for her, based on her selection criteria, and apply to them.

Your child could have her heart set on attending Dartmouth. She could be captivated by the idea of going to college in rural New England, and look forward to small classes and a traditional liberal arts education. The only problem with Dartmouth is that its acceptance rate is 10%. Your child may benefit from considering other colleges that offer a similar setting and programs that your child wants for her college experience. Your child could apply to Colgate University in Upstate New York (26% acceptance rate), and even consider small liberal arts colleges in the Midwest like Grinnell College in Iowa (27% acceptance rate) or Carleton College (23% acceptance rate) in Minnesota. All offer similar small-town and highly regarded liberal arts experiences comparable to those your child would have at Dartmouth.

An applicant interested in attending Duke for one of its excellent science programs and Southern location faces a 9% acceptance rate. This applicant could also consider Wake Forest located close by in Winston Salem, North Carolina (34% acceptance rate), Emory University in Atlanta (27% acceptance rate) or Tulane in New Orleans (27% acceptance rate). These are also small or mid-sized private universities in the South with renowned science programs.

This same logic holds true with public flagship universities. I had a very close friend in high school that was set on attending the University of Virginia. He wanted to leave California and go to a top public university that offered an excellent undergraduate business program, national sports programs with big Saturday football tailgates, and a vibrant Greek scene (fraternities and sororities). Unfortunately he was not accepted to the University of Virginia, which caps the number of students it accepts from out of state. My friend also applied to the University of Michigan, which met all of his college criteria factors, and ultimately attended there. While Michigan was not his first choice, of all the people I know, he probably enjoyed his college experience the most.

2. Consider women's colleges affiliated with selective universities

Your child could also consider women's colleges affiliated with highly selective co-ed colleges that she is interested in attending. Many women's colleges allow their students to enroll in classes or earn a second degree at their co-ed affiliated school. For example, St. Mary's is the women's college affiliated with Notre Dame. Its acceptance rate is almost four times higher than Notre Dame and even offers its students the option to earn an engineering degree from Notre Dame.

Your child may be dismissive to the idea of attending a women's college. However, if the women's college is affiliated with a co-ed school, your child will have plenty of opportunity to interact with students of the opposite sex and participate in activities and take classes on the affiliated college's campus. Scripps College students join clubs on other Claremont College campuses and go to parties hosted by students from the other

Claremont Colleges. A student who attends a women's college affiliated with a co-ed college can take advantage of as many opportunities to engage with the affiliated co-ed college as she wants. If your child is considering any of the following highly selective co-ed colleges, she could also consider their affiliated women's colleges as well.

College	Co-ed Admit Rate	Women's College Admit Rate
Columbia University	6%	Barnard College (20.5%)
The Claremont Colleges	Claremont McKenna (11%); Pomona (12%); Pitzer (13%); Harvey Mudd (14%)	Scripps College (27%)
Notre Dame	21%	Saint Mary's (83%)
Main Line Colleges	Swarthmore (17%); Haverford (24%)	Bryn Mawr (40%)

3. Consider internationally recognized colleges abroad

Your child could also consider attending an internationally recognized university abroad. Canadian colleges including the University of British Columbia (Vancouver) and McGill University (Montreal) are considered among the best universities in the world and offer comparable educations to highly selective colleges in the United States. Many American students attend Canadian colleges and, as foreign students, bring unique perspective to those colleges, which Canadian admissions officers value. Americans attending Canadian colleges usually pay less than what they would expect to pay for private universities in the United States.

Your child could also consider British colleges like St. Andrews University, Oxford, and Cambridge. Gaining admission to these colleges can also be very competitive, but your child will bring relatively unique perspective as an American applicant and therefore demonstrate value to a British college admissions officer. Many top universities in the United Kingdom and Canada accept the SAT. If your child is interested in attending college abroad, you should find out the application requirements and deadlines, as they may be different and much earlier than American colleges.

IV. Application Timing Affects Your Child's Odds of Admission

The timing of your child's application can make a significant impact on her odds of admission. Your child should take advantage of significantly higher odds of admission through an early application program for her top choice college(s), as long as it makes sense financially for your family. This section will discuss different early application programs that colleges offer and how your child should take advantage of them to increase her odds.

Different colleges have different application deadlines. You should make sure your child submits her applications in advance of each college's deadline. The University of California's application deadline is November 30th, while many private universities have an application deadline at the beginning of January.

Your child should not leave submitting her applications to the last minute. Not only are rushed applications more susceptible to errors, but many online college application systems have crashed in the hours leading up to the deadline under the pressure of so many last-minute applications. It is best that your child submits all of her applications at least two days prior to the deadline to ensure that they are submitted successfully online.

1. *Regular Decision*

Regular decision refers to applications that are due as early as the end of November and usually no later than the beginning of January. Regular decision is the normal application process and offers no advantages compared to other application programs a college may offer. If your child plans to apply to a college that offers a priority or preferred application deadline, your child MUST submit her application by the preferred or priority cut-off date. Failing to do so will severely harm your child's odds of admission, as many of the available slots will be allocated before admissions officers review your child's application.

2. *Early Decision*

Early decision is a binding application program, where an applicant agrees to apply to **one** college and submit all application materials by November 1st. Because the application is binding, an applicant that applies early decision is obligated to attend that university and withdraw any outstanding applications to other colleges if she is admitted.

Colleges notify early decision applicants by mid December if they have been accepted, rejected, or deferred to regular decision review by mid December. If an applicant is deferred, it means that applicant will be considered again as part of the regular decision applicant pool and find out by April if she will be admitted to that college.

Some colleges offer an 'Early Decision II' application program in addition to an 'Early Decision I' program. Early Decision II is like an early decision program with a November 1st deadline, but has a January deadline. Early Decision II may be a better fit for an applicant that is able to commit to attend one college but needs additional time to complete the college application, take the SAT an additional time, or submit grades from the first semester of senior year to strengthen her application.

Applying to an early decision application program can more than triple an applicant's odds of acceptance to her dream college when compared to applying regular decision. Below is a list of highly selective colleges that offer early decision application programs, and their rates of admission compiled from these colleges' websites and other online sources. The first column lists the admission rate for students who apply regular decision. The second column lists the admission rate for students who apply early decision. The third column lists the percentage of students of the entering freshman class that applied early decision.

Admission Rates for Selective Colleges Offering Early Decision Programs

College	Admit % (Reg. Decision)	Admit % (Early Decision)	Early Decision / Enrolled %
Columbia University	6%	20%	45%
Brown University	7%	20%	38%
University of Pennsylvania	7%	24%	54%
Claremont McKenna College	8%	26%	54%
Dartmouth College	9%	26%	43%
Duke University	9%	26%	47%
Pomona College	9%	19%	34%
Amherst College	10%	36%	36%
Vanderbilt University	10%	23%	46%

College	Admit % (Reg. Decision)	Admit % (Early Decision)	Early Decision / Enrolled %
Johns Hopkins University	11%	29%	41%
Pitzer College	11%	29%	45%
Northwestern University	11%	36%	50%
Colorado College	12%	27%	42%
Bowdoin College	13%	28%	47%
Tufts University	14%	33%	44%
Swarthmore College	15%	36%	49%
Williams College	15%	41%	44%
Washington University at St. Louis	16%	42%	37%
Washington and Lee College	17%	41%	54%
Bates College	18%	69%	53%
Carleton College	18%	37%	44%
Davidson College	19%	43%	53%
Bucknell University	22%	60%	48%

College	Admit % (Reg. Decision)	Admit % (Early Decision)	Early Decision / Enrolled %
Kenyon College	22%	53%	45%
Haverford College	23%	49%	42%
Bard College	24%	56%	8%
Oberlin College	27%	54%	36%
American University	33%	78%	46%

The difference between early decision and regular decision admission rates is somewhat misleading. Many of the colleges listed above require recruited athletes to apply early decision. Some colleges also require applicants that have alumni legacies to apply early decision if they want their alumni legacies to be considered in the application process.

Even with these favored applicants, applying early decision improves an applicant's odds of admission. In the early decision cycle, all of a college's spots are available whereas some colleges have already filled half of their incoming class spots by the time admissions officers begin reviewing regular decision applicants. Moreover, applicants that apply early decision are guaranteed to protect a college's yield, which makes them more attractive to admissions officers.

Before your child applies early decision to any college, your family must understand the financial implications if she is accepted. Your child is obligated to enroll where she is accepted under an early decision application program and your family will have to find a way to pay for your child's education. While many of these colleges are very expensive, some of them offer the most generous no-loan financial aid packages to students with grants awarded to students whose families earn up to $150,000 per year.

3. *Early Action*

Early action is a nonbinding early application program. With an early action application, an applicant submits her application, usually by the beginning or middle of November, and is notified whether she is accepted, rejected, or deferred to the regular decision applicant pool by the middle of December. If an applicant is accepted under an early action program, she can continue to apply to other colleges and decide by the regular decision deadline whether she will enroll or not.

Single choice early action programs allow applicants to only apply to that college through an early application program. Other early action programs allow applicants to submit as many early action applications as they want, provided the other colleges allow additional early action applications as well.

Below is a list of highly selective colleges that offer an early action application program and their acceptance rates compiled from colleges' websites and other online sources. The first column lists the admission rate for all applicants regardless of the application program they apply with. The second column lists the admission rate for applicants who apply with an early action program.

College	Admit % (Overall)	Admit % (Early Action)
Stanford University	5%	10%
Harvard University	6%	15%
Yale University	6%	17%
Princeton University	7%	18%
MIT	8%	10%
University of Chicago	8%	12%
Cal Tech	9%	13%
University of Notre Dame	21%	30%

The admissions boost for applying early action for some colleges is not as great as the boost for applying early decision. Even if the boost for applying to a college's early action program is not as great, it is still a boost that your child should take advantage of if it applies to one of her top college choices.

4. *Your child should apply early*

Your child should apply either early decision or early action to one of her top choice colleges if it offers an early application program. The difference in acceptance rates between regular and early application programs is too large to ignore. If your child's top choice only offers an early decision application program and your family is concerned with paying that college's cost, your child should apply early action to one of her reach schools that offers a non-binding early action application program. Even if that college is not her top choice, it will increase her odds of gaining admission to it and provide your family with the chance to assess any scholarships or grants before enrolling.

5. *Submit applications as soon as possible to colleges that accept applications on a rolling basis*

Some private and public universities accept applications on a rolling basis. This means that the college will assess applications as they are received and make application decisions on a first come, first serve basis. You should find out if any of the colleges your child plans to apply to accept applications on a rolling basis. If any of them do, your child should apply as soon as your child has completed a compelling application. However, it is better to submit a strong application than a rushed application to take advantage of additional spots and scholarship funds at the beginning of the application period. It is okay if your child needs to take the SAT an additional time and submit an application in November instead of in September. Do not rush an application just because the college makes admission decisions on a rolling basis. The benefit of a stronger application far outweighs its timing.

V. Conclusion

Where and when your child applies to will influence her admissions cycle. By developing objective criteria to select colleges for your child to apply to, and understanding under what circumstances your family is able or willing to pay for certain colleges, your family can help your child draw up an appropriate list of colleges. In drawing up her list, your child should be open minded and apply to colleges that will give her the college experience she wants at a price that makes sense financially for your family. College is what your child will make of it. Applying to the right mix of reach and safety schools will ensure your child enrolls at a college that is a good fit for her. When applying, your child should take advantage of either an early decision or early application program at one of her top choice colleges. Applying early can significantly improve her odds of admission and help your child gain acceptance to one of her top choices for college.

Chapter 10:

Scholarships And Financial Aid

I. Be Open Minded and Diligent to Reduce the Cost of Your Child's College Education

The only part of the college application process that may be more daunting than persuading an admission officer to admit your child is figuring out how to pay for your child's college education. Today, private universities can cost more than $70,000 per year including tuition, fees, room, and board. Public colleges and universities can also be incredibly expensive with some public flagship universities costing over $30,000 per year for tuition, fees, room, and board.

Similar to using strategy to gain admission to highly selective colleges, the high cost of a college education also requires your family to use strategy—in this case, to offset the high costs through merit scholarships and need-based grants. Instead of resigning yourself or your child to taking out six figure loans to pay for college, your family should avail itself of the millions of dollars of scholarships and grants that colleges and outside organizations offer applicants each year.

The most important part of reducing the cost of your child's college education is to keep an open mind with the colleges your child applies to. Your child should consider applying to colleges that offer merit scholarships, especially for safety schools. Many private colleges offer up to full tuition scholarships to applicants at the top of the applicant pool, while public universities can offer compelling out-of-state applicants, in-state tuition rates to drastically reduce the cost of attendance.

You may also be surprised at the income levels that qualify for need-based grants. Some of the most selective colleges have financial aid policies that enable students to graduate debt free and receive no-loan financial aid packages based on demonstrated need. Families earning up to $150,000 may qualify for grants that cover a child's tuition. This Chapter discusses how you and your child should approach college-sponsored merit scholarships, need-based grants, and outside scholarships.

II. Pursue Scholarships and Grants Awarded by Colleges

Many colleges offer merit scholarships to compelling applicants to entice them to enroll and need-based grants to applicants that demonstrate an inability to pay all or part of the cost of their college education. Your family should research the financial aid and scholarship policies of colleges your child is interested in attending. Many of the most selective colleges in the country have similar financial aid policies. For example, Ivy League colleges, Stanford, Williams and other highly selective colleges do not offer merit scholarships. The applicants they admit are some of the most compelling college applicants in the world and many, if not all, would qualify for some form of merit scholarship. However, these highly selective colleges offer generous, no-loan, need-based financial aid programs designed to enable students (and their families) to graduate debt free. At some of these highly selective colleges, over 60% of students receive need-based grants, with the average award amounting to $40,000 (close to the cost of tuition).

Families that earn up to $150,000 per year may qualify for significant grants at highly selective colleges. These financial aid policies should incentivize your child to gain admission to the most selective colleges in the country and also help explain the dramatic increase in the number of applicants for the most selective colleges in the country with generous financial aid policies. If an applicant can earn admission to a highly selective college, she may earn a reduction for much of her cost of attendance through generous grants that the college offers.

By creating a compelling application that persuades admissions officers at highly selective colleges to admit your child, your child could potentially kill two birds with one stone. Through a compelling application, your child may also persuade admissions officers to award her generous merit scholarships. Or, if your child is applying to highly selective colleges that do not offer merit scholarships but instead offer no-loan financial aid, presenting a compelling application may get your child into a college that could offer her hundreds of thousands of dollars of grants based on her demonstrated financial need. Therefore, it is critically important for your child to create a compelling application to gain admission and offset the cost of a college education. Your child will have two ways to reduce the cost of her college education directly from the colleges she applies to: (1) merit-based scholarships and (2) need-based grants.

1. *Merit-Based Scholarships*

Many private colleges offer merit scholarships to entice their most compelling applicants to accept their offers of admission and enroll. Merit scholarships can cover the full cost of tuition, and potentially room, board, and other fees. Your child will not receive merit scholarships if she does not apply to colleges that offer them. Your family should cast a wide net to find colleges that your child would be interested in attending where she may also be a strong contender for a large scholarship.

Merit scholarships are often awarded on the strength of an application and do not require any additional essays or forms. All of the work your child will put into making each component of her college application compelling could translate into significant merit scholarships for her. To increase your child's odds of receiving a merit scholarship from a private college, she can apply to colleges where her entrance exam scores and high school transcript place her at the top of the applicant pool. If a college accepts more than 25% of its applicants and your child is in the top 25% of the applicant pool for all components of the SAT I or ACT and has as close to straight 'A's' as possible, your child will be at the top of that college's applicant pool and potentially be in a strong position for a merit scholarship. Any other component of your child's college application that is also compelling, including your child's extracurricular activities or personal statement, may also lead to a merit scholarship.

Some colleges offer merit scholarships through endowments that require an additional essay or application. If possible, apply to these scholarship programs after your child has found out if she has been accepted. Treat any application for a scholarship like applying to college: your child should demonstrate as much value as possible to persuade an organization that awards scholarships to grant one to your child. Merit scholarships are designed to entice the most compelling applicants to enroll at that college. The more value your child demonstrates, the stronger her odds of receiving a merit scholarship.

Some public and private colleges offer scholarships to recruited athletes as well. As part of your search for recruitment matches, determine if the colleges your child is interested in competing for offer athletic scholarships. Some colleges, including Ivy League colleges, do not offer athletic scholarships, while other smaller colleges that have NCAA Division II athletic programs offer full tuition scholarships for their most coveted recruits. It is important to understand the number of scholarships a college's sport team has to offer. Some teams may only have the equivalent of two or three full tuition scholarships that they must allocate over eight incoming student athletes. The number of scholarships a team has will affect the size of your child's athletic scholarship from a college.

Out-of-state public universities can offer in-state tuition prices for compelling applicants as well. If your child is considering applying to an out-of-state public university as a safety school, she should find out if that university offers any forms of merit scholarship including offering tuition at in-state prices to top applicants.

2. Need-Based Grants

Many public and private colleges offer need-based grants to applicants that demonstrate an inability to pay the full cost of a college education. Need-based grants are based strictly on need. Your child's accomplishments will not be taken into consideration when assessing your family's ability to pay for college. Grants are like scholarships; they reduce the cost of a college education and do no need to be repaid. Colleges require students that will apply for need-based financial aid to complete the Federal Application for Federal Student Aid ('FAFSA') and, depending on the college, a college-specific financial aid application as well.

Before your child applies to any college where she will also apply for financial aid, it is important to understand if the college practices need-blind admissions. Need-blind admissions means it is a college's policy to not take into consideration a student's (in)ability to pay when making admission decisions. If your child plans to apply for financial aid, she should understand that some colleges prefer to admit applicants that can pay for or finance their education through outside lenders. If paying for college will be a challenge for your family, find colleges that practice need-blind admissions.

When applying for need-based financial aid, you and your child should be open minded with colleges that offer need-based grants and the size of the grants your child could receive. As previously discussed, some of the most selective colleges have instituted no-loan financial aid policies where students receive grants that do not need to be repaid, based on demonstrated need. At some of these colleges over half of undergraduate students receive grants, with the average award exceeding $40,000 per year. These grants may cover the full cost of tuition. Some of these colleges advertise that students whose families make up to $150,000 per year receive substantial grants. Other colleges, even if not known for large endowments and no-loan financial aid policies, also offer generous need-based grants. If your family lacks the resources to fully pay for your child's college education and the college practices need-blind admissions, your child should apply for financial aid.

If your child comes from a divorced family, your child should provide the financial information of the parent that has primary custody of your child. If your child splits her time equally with both parents, provide the financial information for the parent that makes less each year and/or has fewer assets if possible. The greater the demonstrated need, the greater the need-based grant. Some colleges may require supplemental reports from both parents after your child has been accepted. Your child should comply with any requests for information from the colleges she applies to and their individual financial aid practices.

III. Negotiate with Colleges Once Your Child Is Accepted

When your child applies to college, it is a seller's market. Colleges boast as many as twenty applicants for every spot in their incoming class. When your child applies to college, she will do everything she can to gain admission. However, after your child has been admitted, the power dynamics shift to a buyer's market that benefits your child. Your child will begin to receive materials from the colleges she earned admission to as these colleges try to convince your child to accept their offers and boost their own yield. As the power dynamic shifts to favor your child, your child will have the ability to negotiate with the colleges that have accepted her to increase the size of her merit scholarships and/or need-based grants.

If your child has been accepted to two or more colleges that have offered her merit scholarships, your child should try to negotiate with the colleges that have offered her smaller merit scholarships to match the highest scholarship offer that your child has received. Your child should tell the admissions officer she will need a larger merit scholarship to be in a financial position to accept the offer based on other merit scholarships she has received. Your child should explain to the admissions officer that she is unable to afford the cost of her college education based on the existing scholarship offer and will attend a college that offered her more scholarship funds unless this college matches her higher offer. It is okay for your child to be a tough negotiator. Your child will not interact with the admissions office after she enrolls at that college or enrolls elsewhere.

Negotiating for additional merit scholarships with a college will be easier if your child can refer to scholarship offers from colleges that are 'peer schools,' or similar, with respect to prestige and admissions selectivity. Your child can refer to U.S. News and World Report's college rankings to assess which colleges are considered peer schools to each other.

Even if your child has received merit scholarships from non-peer schools, your child should still try to create a bidding war among the colleges she has been accepted to. Remember that after a college admits your child, it is competing with other colleges to entice your child to accept its admission offer. Your child has nothing to lose and tens of thousands of dollars or more to gain by negotiating with colleges that have accepted her for additional merit scholarships. Your family may be temped to bluff as to the college that offered your child a scholarship or the amount of the scholarship, but be prepared for admissions officers to ask for documentation that supports a competing scholarship offer.

If another college matches the initial highest merit scholarship, your child should contact the admissions officer of the college that awarded her the initial largest merit scholarship and ask for additional scholarships from that college. Your child should tell the college that offered her the highest initial scholarship that it needs to offer her more scholarship funds for her to attend that college.

Your child can also work with financial aid officers to increase the size of any need-based grant offers that are unsatisfactory. It is possible that additional information about your family's financial circumstances would help financial aid officers reevaluate your family's ability to pay and potentially increase the amount of grants your child receives. If your child has been accepted to a college and receives a less than satisfactory need-based grant, you should immediately set up a phone appointment with the financial aid office to explain your family's financial situation and why your child needs additional grants. You can ask the financial aid officer what you could do so that your child is considered for additional grants. The financial aid officer will provide you with additional instructions for requesting a review and/or increase of her original need-based grants. Increasing your child's need-based grants is a back-and-forth process with the college's financial aid office, but can result in significant increases to the grants your child receives.

Some colleges may offer your child financial aid through loans instead of grants. Your family should not be impressed by loan offers. If your child receives loans as part of a financial aid package, you should attempt to convert these loans to grants. Similar to requesting additional merit scholarships from colleges that initially offered lower merit scholarships, your child can ask any college that provided less need-based grants to match larger grants from other colleges. If one college has determined that your child has demonstrated more financial need than another college, your child should send that college the documentation that supports a larger grant and ask that college to match the larger grant.

IV. Apply for Outside Scholarships

Your child should also apply for scholarships from outside organizations as well. Every dollar of scholarship your child receives will reduce the cost of her college education. There are no limits to the amount of scholarships your child can receive. Your family should start the outside scholarship search in ninth grade. Yes, your child will be very busy creating a compelling profile for her college applications and may not have a lot of time to search for scholarships. However, if your family sets aside one or two hours a month to search for and apply for scholarships, you may be able to offset a significant portion of the cost of your child's college education. Everything your child does to create a compelling profile for the college application process will also create a compelling profile for college scholarship applications.

There are several online resources available to search for outside scholarships. The College Board is a starting point, with an online scholarship search engine that allows your family to search for scholarships based on your child's characteristics and interests. See https://bigfuture. collegeboard.org/scholarship-search. Also, www.scholarships.com is a site exclusively dedicated to finding higher education scholarships. Your child should also ask her high school guidance counselor if any local organizations like Kiwanis or the National Legion offer scholarships to local high school students.

Your family should approach outside scholarships with a strategy to maximize the return on time your family spends searching and applying for them. Highly publicized, national scholarships from large corporations, and endowments that offer tens of thousands of dollars, attract thousands of applications and make your child's odds to receive them very low. Instead, your child should focus on lower profile, niche scholarships that target high school students based on specific characteristics like background, interest, or location. The reduced-level competition for niche scholarships will benefit your child's odds of receiving them and could translate into more scholarships for her. If your child receives several small scholarships over four years, she may surpass the amount of scholarship she would receive from one larger scholarship.

V. Conclusion

Your child should consider applying to schools where she will be a strong contender for receiving merit scholarships and/or need-based grants. By applying to colleges that offer generous merit scholarships or need-based grants, your child has a better chance of covering a large portion of the cost of her college education. Once your child is admitted to college, she will have leverage to negotiate additional scholarships or grants from the colleges that have accepted her. To successfully negotiate increases in scholarships or grants, your child should support her request for additional funds by providing documentation of competing offers she has received from other colleges.

In addition to scholarships and grants from colleges your child will apply to, your family should dedicate time throughout high school for your child to apply to niche scholarships. By spending a few hours a month on applying for scholarships, your child can accumulate numerous smaller scholarships throughout high school that can further reduce the cost of your child's college education.

Chapter 11:

Getting Admitted From The Waitlist

I. What is a Waitlist?

Colleges admit more applicants than the number of spots they have in their incoming freshman classes. Not every admitted applicant will enroll at the college that accepted her. If a college's yield is 50%, fifty percent of the applicants will enroll and 50% will decline their admission offers. However, sometimes fewer students accept admission offers and enroll elsewhere. When the actual yield of admitted students is less than the projected yield, college admissions officers will have available spots in their incoming class.

How do admissions officers fill these available spots? In addition to admitting or rejecting applicants, admissions officers will identify applicants that they would like to admit, but only if there is space available for them. These are compelling applicants, but, due to the limited size of a college class, will only receive admission offers if a college's actual yield is less than its projected yield. College admission officers place these compelling applicants on a waitlist, and offer them spots if they become available after all of the admitted students accept or decline their admission offers.

Being on a waitlist is an undesirable position to be in. While it is somewhat flattering to know that a college's admissions office would like to admit your child, it still stings to not gain outright admission. The uncertainty of whether your child will ultimately gain admission to a school that has placed her on a waitlist can be grueling on your entire family as the summer drags on and your child makes plans to attend another college.

Your child may be offered a spot on the waitlist for a college, but decide that she would rather attend another school that has already made her an offer. If this is the case, your child does not need to try to get off the waitlist. However, your child may be placed on the waitlist at her dream college or put on the waitlist of a college where admission would be the best possible outcome for your child.

To earn admission from the waitlist, your child will have to convince admissions officers that she is a compelling applicant that will add more value to the college than the other applicants on the waitlist. This Chapter discusses the strategy your child should use for gaining admission to a college from the waitlist.

II. Understand How the Waitlist Works

The size of a waitlist and number of students admitted from it varies from college to college and from year to year. Your child should find out how many students the college placed on the waitlist and how many applicants are usually admitted from the waitlist. Your child can find this information online or from the college's admission office.

Some colleges rank waitlisted applicants when they place them on the waitlist and offer admission to the highest-ranked applicants. For example, if there are 250 applicants on the waitlist, and fifty spots become available for the incoming freshman class, the top fifty applicants will receive offers of admission. If any applicants withdraw from the waitlist or decline an admission offer, admissions officers will extend offers to lower ranked applicants on the waitlist until they fill the incoming class.

Other college admissions offices do not rank their waitlists. After determining how many spots are available in their incoming class, admissions officers at these colleges will review all of the waitlisted applicants' applications an additional time and extend offers to students that add the most value to that college. Regardless of how a waitlist is organized, your child should supplement her application with limited and strategic additions that demonstrate the value she can add to the college.

III. Make the Hard Sell to Get Off the Waitlist

Consider the following strategies that applicants have successfully used to earn admission from the waitlist in the past:

1. *Send a letter of continued interest*

Your child should send a one-page letter of continued interest to the admissions office of any college that placed her on a waitlist. A letter of continued interest accomplishes two things. First, it signals that your child will attend that college if admitted, and therefore demonstrates that your child will protect that college's yield. Second, the letter of continued interest can highlight any accomplishments, awards, or experiences your child has gained since applying to that college that demonstrate additional value.

Alternatively, if your child has a unique skill like poetry or film, she could consider highlighting this skill to make the pitch to be admitted off the waitlist. Keep the poem, video, painting, etc. short and sweet (so it is the equivalent to a one-page letter) and make sure it conveys the value your child will add to the college.

If your child is placed on a college's waitlist, she should find out how she can send additional materials to the admissions office for consideration. Your child should call the admissions office and see if it accepts additional material electronically or via the mail. Make sure that anything your child sends to the admissions office includes her application reference number and complies with any additional instructions the admission office has for submitting additional materials.

In the letter of continued interest, your child must state that she will attend that college if accepted. Your child's assertion will be more credible if she refers to specific programs at the college that she is excited about. When referring to a college's specific programs, your child should also demonstrate that she will add value to those programs based on her own skills, interests, or experiences. The letter of continued interest is your child's last chance to make a 'hard sell' to an admissions officer on the value she will add to that college.

In addition to referring to specific college programs that your child could contribute to, your child should also inform the college admissions officers of any notable achievements since she submitted her application, such as a relevant award, contribution to a breakthrough at a science lab, or how she led a successful community service project. It is not a time to be bashful. Your child should use her accomplishments to demonstrate value to try and earn admission to one of the few remaining spots.

Example letter of continued interest:

April 2, 2016
Harvard College Admissions
Harvard College
5 James St, Cambridge, MA 02138

Dear Harvard College Admissions Committee,

Thank you for the opportunity to be on the waitlist for the Class of 2021. I am writing this letter to express my continued interest and to confirm that I would be delighted to attend Harvard this fall should I be offered the opportunity. Harvard is my top choice for my college education.

I would welcome the opportunity to add to the diverse and talented incoming freshman class at Harvard. Since my application last fall, I have remained dedicated to developing leadership and advocacy for the disenfranchised in my community as President of The Education Coalition in San Diego. This past February, we launched our first computer-skills boot camp for students whose access to computers is very limited. We designed a curriculum, and trained thirty middle school students at risk of failing seventh and eighth grade, on how to use computer hardware and software to enhance their education. Our goal was to inspire these students to remain in school and give them additional resources to succeed.

As President of Education Coalition, I partnered with Mega Computers to secure fifteen laptops for our mobile classroom and organized a team of twelve high school tutors to teach our boot-camp participants. Our participants are now more connected to their community and able to take advantage of additional educational opportunities. We are now working to expand the boot camp to teach more participants next year.

My experience leading Education Coalition has strengthened my abilities as a leader and given me the confidence to partner with large companies on important projects that benefit my community. I have also learned how to organize a complicated event with many participants.

I would be delighted to join the freshman class at Harvard in the fall and apply my advocacy and leadership skills within the college. In particular, I would welcome the opportunity to be an integral part of the Harvard Refugee Assistance Project. I look forward to hearing from you.

Sincerely,

Greg Kaplan

Analysis:

1. This letter is addressed to the Harvard Admissions Office the day after admissions decisions are typically sent. While colleges wait to see how many students accept their admissions offers, your child should demonstrate her strong interest in attending the college as soon as possible.

2. I wrote that Harvard is my top choice and I will attend if accepted. I protect the admissions officer's yield and increase my attractiveness as a waitlisted applicant.

3. I do not try to pass myself off as the greatest thing since sliced bread. I recognize the talent of the incoming class and my aspirations to join them. Instead, I focus on the value I would add to Harvard as a student leader.

4. As in an ideal personal statement, I focus on one experience that has happened in the months since I applied to college and its significance to me and the college. I try to demonstrate the value I would bring to Harvard based on this experience. I discuss my accomplishment, and what it means to me as a leader. I tie the experience to Harvard by discussing my plan to join a specific program at Harvard.

This is the type of letter I wish I sent to Harvard when I was waitlisted there. I did not follow up with a letter of continued interest. A letter of continued interest may separate your child from the rest of the applicants on a waitlist and earn your child admission. Do not squander the opportunity.

2. Send an additional letter of recommendation that shows a different side of your child

If your child is placed on the waitlist at a college that requires letters of recommendation as part of the college application, your child should ask an additional recommender to write on her behalf to that college. At this point in the college application process, your child will already have submitted letters of recommendation from two teachers and a guidance counselor. Your child should ask a recommender who could show a different side of your child to college admissions officers. Consider a recommender from outside the classroom like a supervisor from a lab or summer internship, or a community organizer that your child has served with.

Your child should explain to this recommender that she is on a waitlist for one of her top choice colleges and wants to show the type of person she is outside of the classroom based on her experience with the recommender. Your child should provide the additional recommender with her application reference number and mailing instructions for the letter. Your child should also provide the recommender with the same information she provided to her teachers and guidance counselor to give the recommender context to write a more insightful letter.

When I was waitlisted at Harvard and Yale, I asked the superintendent of my school district to write letters to those schools. I was one of three elected student representatives (out of more than 12,000 students) to my district's school board and worked closely with the superintendent. I wanted to include a letter in my application that showcased my involvement in an important government organization and highlight a unique experience that demonstrated valuable perspective and leadership. Even though I was ultimately not accepted at either school, I made an effort to demonstrate additional value to both schools' admissions offices when they reviewed my application an additional time.

3. Consider a visit and in-person meeting with your child's assigned admission officer

If your child is waitlisted at a college that is close to your home, or you will be touring another college that is near by, your child could make an appointment with her assigned admissions officer at that college to deliver an in-person pitch. The cost of a long drive or flight may not be worth it, but if it is relatively easy and inexpensive to meet with an admissions officer, your child could take the opportunity to stand out from the other waitlisted applicants.

If your child schedules an in-person meeting with her assigned admissions officer, she should treat the meeting like a sales pitch where she must demonstrate (1) that she is committed to attending that college and (2) the value she would bring to that school if admitted. Your child can discuss what she included in her letter of continued interest and anything else that would demonstrate the value she would bring to that college.

III. Conclusion

Your child can earn admission from the waitlist by being proactive and demonstrating additional value that she would bring to that college. If your child is placed on a waitlist, she should spare no effort in trying to secure one of the spots that become available. Your child should submit a letter of continued interested that demonstrates her commitment to attending that college and the value she would bring. If the college accepts letters of recommendations, your child should also submit an additional letter of recommendation that shows a different side of your child that, once again, highlights her value. Your child could also consider an in-person meeting with her assigned admissions officer to stand out from the other waitlisted applicants if this feasible for your family.

Conclusion

By demonstrating value in each component of the college application, your child will stand out from other applicants. If your child gives admissions officers the added value to their college that they are looking for as they construct a well-rounded, diverse class that can propel the college forward, she may earn admission to her dream college. Your child has the ability to succeed in this process.

To conclude, the checklist below summarizes the different components of the college application and how your child can demonstrate value with each component.

I. Checklist for Persuading a College Admissions Officer to Admit your Child

1. High school transcript

☐ Excel: earn as many 'A's' as possible in the most challenging courses offered at your child's high school.
☐ Play defense. 'A's' are your child's to lose.
☐ Consider college courses to stand out.
☐ Develop proficiency in a foreign language.

2. Entrance exams

☐ Take the PSAT and PLAN sophomore year as diagnostic and junior year to participate in the National Merit Scholarship Program.
☐ Find the appropriate entrance exam prep program. Start prepping the second half of sophomore year or, at the latest, the summer before junior year.
☐ Take the SAT I / ACT junior year. Retake if necessary.
☐ Target SAT / ACT scores that place your child in the top 25% of the applicant pool for each component of the test for the colleges your child is interested in attending.
☐ Take SAT II subject tests in advanced courses your child takes at the end of the school year for that subject.

3. Theme

☐ Make sure your child's application theme is supported by her high school transcript, entrance exam scores, extracurricular activities, personal statements, responses to form questions, and letters of recommendation.
☐ Use the application theme to tie the different application components together.

4. Extracurricular activities

☐ Keep track of your child's accomplishments.
☐ Encourage your child to pursue her passions.
☐ Focus on quality not quantity.
☐ Demonstrate value as a potential leader and highly skilled member of a school-sponsored program.
☐ Sports recruitment: consider less prominent teams (NCAA Division II schools) for widely played sports or sports that are less popular (i.e. crew or squash).
☐ Clubs and service organizations: your child must be a leader.

- ☐ Consider internships and international experiences consistent with your child's higher education plans.
- ☐ Find opportunities for your child to showcase her accomplishments through rankings, contests, and awards.
- ☐ Use (parenthetical citations) on the application form to educate admissions officers of your child's accomplishments and the value she would bring to college.

5. Personal statements

- ☐ Proofread and conform to any word limits.
- ☐ Focus on one particular instance and its significance to your child. Show perspective, tie the importance or perspective gained from the instance to college, and demonstrate how the experience and perspective add value to the colleges your child is applying to.
- ☐ Use a title and an attention-grabbing hook.

6. Responses to application form questions

- ☐ Provide strategic answers to form questions that demonstrate your child's value and reinforce her application theme.
- ☐ Select a major consistent with your child's application theme and/or a major that will increase your child's odds of admission.
- ☐ Address any demographic issues.

7. Letters of recommendation

- ☐ Provide recommenders with information about your child that will enable them to write a great recommendation.
- ☐ Choose recommenders consistent with your child's applicant theme.
- ☐ Give recommenders enough time to write their letters and confirm the letters were submitted by the deadline.

8. Interview

☐ Use the interview as an opportunity to demonstrate the value your child will bring to the college.

II. Application Strategy Checklist to Increase Your Child's Odds of Admission to a College that is Good Fit for your Child

1. Selecting colleges to apply to

☐ Develop objective criteria, based on your child's preferences and family's conditions for paying for college, to set the list of reach and safety schools your child will apply to.
☐ Find colleges that offer the college experience your child seeks and that admit more applicants.

2. Application timing

☐ Apply early decision or early action to one of your child's top-choice colleges, taking into consideration your family's ability to commit to paying for that college.
☐ Submit applications to colleges that accept applications on a rolling basis as soon as your child completes a compelling application.

3. Obtaining scholarships and need-based grants

☐ Be open minded to considering colleges that offer merit scholarships and need-based grants.
☐ Apply for outside scholarships. Dedicate a few hours each month to search for, and apply to, outside scholarships. Focus on niche scholarships with less competition.

4. Earning admission from the waitlist

☐ If placed on a waitlist, demonstrate value to a college admissions officer through a letter of continued interest and an additional letter of recommendation that shows a different side of your child.

☐ Consider an in-person meeting with the assigned admission officer if easily accessible.

III. Parting Thoughts

When your child receives her acceptance letters, it will be an accomplishment that speaks to years of hard work in and out of the classroom. Your child should be recognized for her effort. You, the parent, should also be recognized for inspiring your child to succeed and for providing your child with the confidence, resources and skills to grow into a talented and promising young adult. As I wrote in the introduction, if your biggest concern as a parent is whether your child will earn admission to Duke or Northwestern, you have succeeded wildly as a parent.

Your child may also receive rejection letters at the end of the college application process. Your child may apply to a college that accepts a fraction of its applicants and will be competing with some of the most talented and accomplished students from around the world for admission. Even if your child does everything right—earns straight A's, aces the SAT, boasts compelling extracurricular achievements and writes an insightful personal statement—she may still not earn admission to her dream college. The competition is fierce. It may not seem like it when reading this book, or even when a dreaded rejection email arrives in your child's inbox, but trust me: COLLEGE AND LIFE WILL WORK OUT FOR YOUR CHILD.

I will give you one final example from my own life. When I was a junior in high school, I developed a 'mild' obsession with Princeton. My family would say it was much more severe, but I am sticking with my side of the story. My Mom and I had driven up from Philadelphia after trying to find Penn and getting scared off by the neighborhood and our inability to find parking. We blew off Penn and went to the King of Prussia Mall. While being dragged from store to store—and there are *so many* stores there—I began to reconsider applying to the Ivy League, which had been my destiny since I declared in a first grade show-and-tell that I would attend Harvard like my childhood hero, John F. Kennedy.

I loved everything about Princeton. I salivated at the opportunity to study creative writing with my then-favorite author, Toni Morrison. I loved the gothic architecture and residential college system. I pictured myself playing golf on the course adjacent campus. Finally, and at the time the most important, as a kid who grew up in Arizona and Southern California, it was a balmy 55 degrees on a sunny day in early April when we visited. The good weather on my visit convinced me that New Jersey was much more hospitable than the New England schools I had visited in the dead of winter. So, I bought a sweatshirt from the campus bookstore and envisioned myself studying at Princeton for an entire year.

It didn't work out. I was deferred in the early decision round. I kept up hope of earning admission in the regular decision round—until my Dad called me at the end of March with news that I had received a small envelope in the mail from Princeton, which in the days of when college admissions offices contacted you by mail, was a euphemism for a rejection letter. This was one of the first times I had been rejected from anything in my life, and I was crushed. Almost ten years has gone by since getting that call and I shake my head when I think about how dramatic I was about being rejected. If only I knew then that getting rejected from Princeton was good for me. I ended up at the right college for *me*.

You may think that I deserve no sympathy. You are right and I ask for none. I was accepted to an incredible college that I was meant to attend. Instead of feeling sorry for myself for not studying creative writing at Princeton, I moved on. At Penn I worked my butt off my freshman year to transfer into the Wharton School of Business and ultimately earned a degree in finance. I mastered Spanish and spent half of my junior year studying in Argentina.

While living in Argentina, I decided on a whim to take a 27-hour bus ride to Brazil. The trip was not a success. Almost immediately upon arriving in Brazil, I was held up at gunpoint and, in my panic, became lost and unable to find my way back to the border. I thought I would be able to communicate in Spanish with Brazilians and that we would understand each other enough for me to figure out where I needed to go to get to safety. That was not the case and many hours later, fearing for my safety, I finally found the border and illegally crossed back to my adopted homeland. On the journey home, I decided that I would learn Portuguese and never be so helpless again. When I returned to Penn I enrolled in as many Portuguese classes as I could and became fluent in Portuguese by the time I graduated.

I secured a summer internship at an international investment bank after getting the bankers interviewing me to laugh about my adventures and misfortune in South America. I then moved to New York using the Chinatown Bus. Two weeks into my internship, one of the senior bankers found out I spoke Spanish and I was transferred to Mexico City. As a college intern, I was the official presence for the bank in Mexico. After graduating, I launched a career in private equity in the United States and, of all places, Brazil. My college experience was what I made it. I made Penn into my dream college because I followed my interests and passions. Your child can make her college experience whatever she wants it to be.

I didn't want to go to Penn when I was accepted. I couldn't even find Penn when I tried to visit it. However, at Penn I learned first-hand that anything was possible if I set my mind to it. My college experience, at a college I almost did not apply to, shaped the person I am today.

Your child's college experience will also shape her into the person she is destined to be. Whether it is at Penn or Penn State, your child will learn that anything is possible for her if she has the will and vision to achieve it. Even if your child does not have the outcome she envisions with the college application process, she will succeed in college and beyond. No matter what college your child attends, she will develop academic interests and real world skills, make friends for life, and grow into a capable adult ready to make her mark on the world. Success in the college application process is not measured by acceptances and rejections, but rather your child's growth in college and preparation for the world beyond it. Your child's college education will be one of many accomplishments to come. I wish you and your child the best of luck.

APPENDIX:

College Admissions Timeline

Throughout High School (Ongoing)	
Ongoing	- Make sure your child is earing the best grades in as many advanced classes as possible - Play defense with 'A's'
Ongoing	Build a compelling application theme. Classes, entrance exams, and extracurricular activities should add to the application theme
Ongoing	Develop skills, interests, and passions that are valuable to college admissions officers
Ongoing	Apply for niche scholarships

Summer Before Ninth Grade	
Pre-ninth grade	Make sure your child is enrolled in classes that will enable her to take advanced classes in high school

Ninth Grade	
Most Important	Most Important Encourage your child to pursue her passions and develop as a leader
August	
September	
October	Take the PSAT and PLAN
November	
December	
January	
February	
March	Determine summer plans: consider internships, community service, summer school, and international experiences
April	
May	
June	Begin researching SAT/ACT prep programs (private tutors may fill up years in advance)
July	

Tenth Grade	
Most Important	Find (and begin) SAT/ACT prep program
August	
September	
October	Take PSAT and PLAN
November	
December	
January	Find SAT/ACT prep program, potentially start prep program
February	
March	Determine summer plans: SAT/ACT prep, internships, community service, summer school, college courses, and international experiences
April	
May	SAT II offered
June	SAT II offered Potentially start SAT/ACT Prep
July	

Eleventh Grade	
Most Important	Score in the top 25% of the SAT/ACT range for the colleges your child wants to attend
August	
September	ACT offered
October	- Take PSAT for the National Merit Scholarship Program - SAT I offered; ACT offered
November	SAT I & II offered
December	SAT I & II offered; ACT offered
January	Contact coaches, performing arts and skill based program directors at colleges your child is interested in attending
February	ACT offered
March	- SAT I & II offered - Determine summer plans: SAT/ACT prep, internships, community service, summer school, college courses, and international experiences
April	ACT offered
May	SAT I & II offered
June	SAT I & II offered; ACT offered

Eleventh Grade	
July	NCAA Division 1 athletes may contact prospective athletes - Identify colleges your child will apply to - Begin to brainstorm personal statement ideas that reinforce your child's application theme

Twelfth Grade	
Most Important	Use strategy and marketing to persuade an admissions officer to admit your child!
August	- Ask recommenders to write on your child's behalf; provide information/context to recommenders - Create timeline with application due dates
September	- ACT offered - Create College Board account and begin applications
October	SAT I & II offered; ACT offered -Finalize list of colleges your child will apply to
November	- Early decision and early action applications due; UC applications due -SAT I & II offered
December	Early decision and early action application decisions released
January	- Most regular decision applications due - Make sure the application theme is compelling

Twelfth Grade	
February	
March	
April	Regular decision admissions decisions released - Negotiate merit scholarships and financial aid awards with colleges - If placed on the waitlist: write letter of continued interest; ask for additional letter of recommendation; consider in-person visit with admissions officer
May	- Seat deposits due
June	
July	

More Information

For more information and college application strategy tips, please visit www.earningadmission.com. Please let us know about your child's successes and experience with this book.

If you are interested in working with Greg on your child's college application strategy, please email him at greg@earningadmission.com.

44966343R00092

Made in the USA
San Bernardino, CA
28 January 2017